MW01520180

TRAIN YOUR PUPPY

A Practical and Effective Training Manual that Teaches You How To Literally Hack Your Puppy's Brain to Make Him Do Anything You Want. Even If You Don't Think You Can Do It.

*By **Lucy Chen***

2

TABLE OF CONTENTS

Introduction

The treasure in making and training your dog, everything is contained in this book **TRAIN YOUR PUPPY**: *A Practical and Effective Training Manual that Teaches You How To Literally Hack Your Puppy's Brain to Make Him Do Anything You Want. Even If You Don't Think You Can Do It.* Brace yourself. There is still a Lot of important Information to learn.

The Train your puppy guide for dog owners is a manual all you have to do is read, assimilate and then implement.

CHAPTER ONE

BE READY TO RECEIVE YOUR PUPPY

Some first-time pup proprietors are astounded when they find their new friend nibble, bark, bite, burrow, and messes the house with pee and excrement. However, these are largely impeccably typical characteristic and essential doggy practices.

Your newcomer is only tingling to learn human house habits. He needs to if it's not too much trouble, yet he needs to realize how to go about things.

It is horrible keeping house activities a mystery. Someone needs to tell the young dog. Also, that someone is you.

Before welcoming a little dog to share your life, without a doubt it is just insightful and reasonable to discover previously what you may anticipate from an ordinary dog, which practices and characteristics you think would be unsuitable? And how to adjust the puppy's wrong conduct and disposition in like manner.

In particular, trainers need to realize how to show the youngling were to take out, what to bite, when to bark, were to burrow, to sit when welcoming individuals, to walk serenely, to settle down etc.

And to shush when mentioned, to suppress his generally gnawing conduct, and to altogether appreciate the organization of different individuals— particularly kids, men, and outsiders.

In the case of choosing your forthcoming little dog from an expert raiser or from a family reproducing a litter for the absolute first time, the criteria are the equivalent.

Search for small dogs raised inside around human friendship and its impact—explicitly around individuals who have committed quality of time to the young dogs' training.

Your little dog should be set up for the clatter of regular residential living—the commotion of the vacuum cleaner, pots and dish dropping in the kitchen, football match-ups shouting on the TV, youngsters crying, and grown-ups contending.

Evaded little dogs that have been brought up in an open-air or pet house. Keep in mind, you need a dog to share your home, so search for a little dog that has been brought up in a home. Cellar and pet house raised young dogs are surely not pet-quality mutts.

They are "domesticated animals" comparable to veal calves and battery hens. They are neither housetrained nor mingled, and they don't make great colleagues. Search for litters that have been brought up in a kitchen or family room.

Picking a breed is exceptionally close to home decision—your decision. Come what may, you will spare yourself a lot of redundant issues and disaster if your choice is a trained and instructed one.

Pick the breed you like, explore breed-explicit characteristics and concerns, and afterward examine the ideal approach to raise and prepare your little dog. Ensure you test drive a few grown-up mutts of your chose breed or type before you settle on your last decision.

Test driving grown-up mutts will rapidly show you all that you have to think about a particular kind. Test driving adult puppies will likewise pinpoint holes in your instruction about dog conduct and preparing.

Despite your decision, kindly don't mess with yourself that you will get a "great" grown-up hound basically by choosing the "great" breed and the "great" singular pup.

Any little dog can turn into a heavenly friend if fittingly mingled and prepared. What's more, regardless of what the breed or reproducing, any little dog can likewise turn into a doggy reprobate if not appropriately handled.

It would be ideal if you make an intelligent look into the decision while choosing your young dog, yet recall: proper socialization and preparing is the single most significant factor deciding how intently the puppy will move toward your perspective on flawlessness in adulthood.

Regardless of your inevitable decision—achievement or disappointment is altogether in your grasp. Your little dog's conduct and personality currently depend totally on great farming and preparing.

Your young dog's living quarters should be planned so that housetraining and chew toy preparing are errorless. Each error is a potential debacle since it paves way for more to come.

Long haul control keeps your young dog from figuring out how to commit errors around the house and enables your little dog to instruct himself to utilize a proper act, to settle down discreetly and smoothly, and to bite fitting chew toys.

Control with chew toys loaded down with kibble and treats shows your young dog to appreciate his conversation and sets him up for those occasions when he may be not be really paid attention to at home.

Observe momentary close constrainment likewise to keep your little dog from committing errors around the house, while enabling your pup to instruct himself to settle down unobtrusively and be tranquil, and the need to bite proper chew toys.

Also, momentary repression empowers you to precisely anticipate when your little dog needs to ease herself, with the goal that you may take your young dog to a fitting latrine territory and prize her for utilizing it.

The skill of active housetraining centers around having the option to anticipate when your pup needs to do whatever it needs to do.

From the minute you pick your dog, there are some extensive criticality concerning socialization and preparations. There is no opportunity to squander. Fundamentally, a grown-up dog's disposition and conduct propensities (both great and awful) are formed during puppyhood—early puppyhood.

Some pups are well on their approach to destroy when they are only two months old. It is particularly simple to commit repulsive errors while choosing a little dog and during his initial days at home.

Such errors, as a rule, have a permanent impact, affecting your puppy's conduct and demeanor for a mind-blowing remainder. It is not necessarily the case that undeveloped eight-week-old little dogs can't be restored. They can if you work rapidly.

In any case, while it's anything but difficult to keep conduct and demeanor issues from the earliest starting point, restoration can be both troublesome and tedious, and it is far-fetched that your little dog will at any point become the grown-up hound you could have loved.

Figure out how to settle on smart decisions while choosing your puppy. Figure out how to execute a course of errorless housetraining and errorless chew toy-preparing the minute your little dog lands at her new home.

Any house soiling or biting error you enable your little dog to make is total unreasonableness, preposterousness because you are making bunches of future pains for yourself, and reality since a large number of puppies are euthanized every year basically because their trainers have no clue on how to housetrain or chew toy-train them.

Even though these small defecations cause little harm in themselves, they set the trend for your young dog's decision of toys and toilets for a long time to come.

You shouldn't treat any young dog's house dirtying or house obliteration botch as a potential debacle, since it predicts various future mix-ups from a puppy with bigger bladder and guts and significantly more dangerous jaws.

Numerous trainers start to see their young dog's damaging tendency when he is four to five months old when the little dog is typically consigned outside. Devastation is the result of a bit of a dog's fatigue, absence of supervision, and a quest for stimulation.

Natural curiosity prompts the forlorn puppy to burrow, bark, and getaway.

Before you search for your ideal young dog, you have to realize what kind of puppy to search for, where to get it, and when to get it. An informed decision is commonly far superior to a rash little dog's purchase.

Also, you have to acquaint yourself with the formative cutoff times thoroughly; they become earnest and vital the day you select your pup. Take as much time as necessary to survey this booklet, watch various young dog classes, and afterward settle on an attentive decision. Your puppy's future relies upon it.

Before you select your little dog (for the most part at about two months of age), you have to realize how to choose a decent reproducer and how to choose a suitable pup. In particular, you have to understand how to evaluate your little dog's social improvement.

By about two months of age, your dog probably becomes altogether familiar with a physical home condition, particularly to a wide range of possibly terrifying commotions.

Your little dog should as of now have been dealt with by numerous individuals, particularly men, youngsters, and outsiders; your pup's flawless housetraining and chew toy training ought to be in progress, and your puppy should as of now have a simple comprehension of essential habits.

In any event, your dog should come, sit, rests, and turn over when called or signaled to. In anticipation of family unit living, the litter of puppies probably been raised inside and around individuals and not in some detached lawn or extravagant pet house.

You need to be assured that a flaw-free housetraining, as well as a chew toy-preparing program, is established the entire first day your young dog gets home.

This is so significant during the first week when little dogs naturally adapt positive or negative propensities that set the trend for quite a long time, months, and in some cases, a very long time to come.

The Critical Period of Socialization finishes by a quarter of a year of age! This is the crucial formative stage during which pups figure out how to acknowledge and appreciate the organization of different dogs and individuals.

Subsequently, your young dog should be associated with individuals when he is twelve weeks old. Be that as it may, since his arrangement of dog vaccination infusions is deficient now, a youthful little dog needs to meet individuals in the security of his own home.

As a general guideline, your young dog needs to have met in any event a hundred distinct individuals before he is two months old and afterward meet an extra hundred individuals during his first month at home.

Also, to the fact that this is simpler to do than it may sound, it's likewise fun.

Nibble hindrance is the absolute most significant exercise a dog must learn. Grown-up hounds have teeth and jaws that can damage and cause mischief.

All creatures must figure out how to hinder the utilization of their weapons against their very own sort. However, social creatures must figure out how to be delicate with all, particularly individuals.

Residential dogs must figure out how to repress their gnawing toward all beings, particularly towards different puppies.

CHAPTER TWO

THE BEST PUPPY BREED TO RAISE

No doubts the greatest formative cutoff time precedes you even start your quest in getting yourself the best pup: to be specific, your training about your little dog. Similarly, as you would figure out how to drive before setting off in a vehicle yourself, you ought to figure out how to raise and prepare a little dog before you get one.

A few trainers expect paradise and earth from their little dogs; others request enchantment and wonders. Some expect the dog to be splendidly respectful and to busy herself when not paid attention to at home for a considerable length of time. What's more, they accept the little dog will mysteriously grow up to acting along these lines without direction.

It is not reasonable to keep house management hidden from your dog, possibly to groan and moan when she typically discovers doggy approaches to engage herself and defy norms she didn't know existed.

If you have house rules, someone needs to instruct them to the little dog. What's more, that someone is you. Fortunately, hounds have their regular action tops at first light and sunset, that such a large number of are happy to settle down and nap the day away. In any case, a few mutts are not. A few dogs are just more dynamic than others, and when disregarded at home, become exceedingly pushed and may pulverize the house and nursery over about a day. Pup proprietors are frequently astonished when their new little dog nibbles, barks, bites, burrows, and finishes the floors with pee and defecation. However, this is the thing that dogs do. How did you anticipate that your puppy would act? To wash? To clean? What's more, what did you expect that your dog would do to take a break of day? Housework? To wipe and clean floors and residue the furnishings? Or, on the other hand, to divert herself understanding books, sitting in front of the TV, or doing macramé?

A Jack Russell

Terrier

PITBULL

MOTHER ROTTWEILER AND PUPPY

Numerous proprietors give off an impression of being at a further misfortune when defied by absolutely unsurprising issues, for example, bouncing up, pulling on-rope, and communicating the unfathomable vitality and extravagance going with doggy puberty.

Furthermore, proprietors are distrustful if their youthful or grown-up hound nibbles or battles. When mutts are under socialized, badgering, mishandled, scared, or generally vexed, what do we anticipate that they should do?

Call a legal counselor? They chomp! Gnawing is as typical an element of a puppy conduct as swaying the tail or crunching a bone.

Before welcoming a little dog to share your life, doubtlessly it is just astute and reasonable for discover beforehand what you may anticipate.

To start with, kindly don't mess with yourself that you should choose the "great" breed and the "great" singular young dog, and he will consequently grow up into the "great" grown-up hound. Any little dog can turn into a heavenly friend if duly mingled and prepared.

What's more, regardless of what his breed or reproducing, any young dog can turn into a doggy reprobate if not appropriately combined and arranged. It will be ideal if you make a wise, investigated decision while choosing your little dog, however, recall: proper socialization and preparing is the single most significant factor deciding how intently the puppy will move toward your perspective on flawlessness in adulthood.

Second thing, look for guidance from the best sources. Normal errors are to take breed counsel from veterinarians, wellbeing exhortation from reproducers, and terrifically significant conduct and to prepare advice from veterinarians, raisers, and pet-store staff.

What's more, if you genuinely need to comprehend what's happening, look at a nearby young dog class and talk with the proprietors; they'll give you the cold, hard actualities in regards to what it truly is to live with a little dog.

Third, look for exhortation from a few sources and assess all guidance cautiously. Apply the excellent judgment standard: does it sound useful to you? Is the counsel pertinent to your family and your way of life? Though some exhortation may sound immaterial, two-faced, redundant, or sketchy. What's more, sporadically "counsel" which can be out and out terrible.

Model 1: One raiser told a couple they couldn't purchase a little dog except if they had a fenced yard, and one of them was home throughout the day.

However, the reproducer herself had no fenced yard, and her twenty or so hounds lived in cases in a pet house at a decent forty yards from her home and any expectation of human friendship. Duh!??

Model 2: Many individuals are advised not to get a significant puppy once they live in a condo. Actually! For whatever length of time that they get customary strolls, massive mutts make superb condo sidekicks. Contrasted and littler puppies and massive mutts regularly settle down better and bark less.

Numerous little puppies bother proprietors and neighbors by being dynamic, loud and running amuck. Littler mutts make magnificent condo associates be that as it may, insofar as they are prepared to settle down and shush.

Model 3: Many veterinarians prompt that Golden Retrievers and Labrador Retrievers are the best puppies with kids. All types of a puppy can make great allies for youngsters, given that they have been prepared the proper behavior around kids, and gave that the kids have been instructed the appropriate etiquette around hounds!

Something else, hounds—including Goldens and Labs—are probably going to be alarmed and bothered by youngsters, or energized and affected by their tricks.

Keep in mind, and you are choosing a pup to live with you for a decent lengthy timespan. Picking a puppy to share your life is exceptionally close to home decision—your decision.

You will spare yourself a ton of pointless issues and awfulness if your choice is educated and a taught one.

In all actuality, however, individuals only sometimes pay regard to benevolent persuasion and as a rule, wind up picking with their emotions rather than their head.

In reality, numerous individuals wind up picking a dog similarly as they would pick a long-lasting human friend: because of coat shading, adaptation, and adorableness.

In any situation, paying little concentration to the numerous purposes behind choosing a specific young dog—regardless of whether family, adjustments, adorableness, or general wellbeing the achievement of the undertaking eventually depends mostly on the puppy's instruction concerning proper conduct and preparing.

All things considered, because of the absence of inbreeding, blended breeds are more beneficial hereditary stock; they will, in general, live more and have fewer medical issues.

Then again, at a pure breed pet house, it is conceivable to look at the neighborliness, essential habits, and general wellbeing.

I am certainly restricted to recommending breeds for individuals. Suggesting specific strains may seem like a supportive and innocuous exhortation.

However, it is deceptively hazardous and not to the most significant advantage of puppies or dog-owning families. Persuasion, either possibly in support of specific breeds regularly persuades that preparation is either redundant or inconceivable. In this way, numerous poor mutts grow up without instruction.

Breed proposals frequently lead clueless trainers to accept that once they have chosen the correct breed, there is nothing more to do.

Thinking they have the ideal kind, numerous proprietors endure the misguided judgment that preparation is redundant, thus try not to. This is the time things start going downhill.

Considerably all the more upsetting, when certain breeds are prescribed, different breeds are naturally being prompted against. "Specialists" regularly recommend that strains are too vast; excessively little, excessively dynamic, excessively lazy, excessively quick, excessively moderate, excessively brilliant, or excessively imbecilic, and like this too hard to even consider training.

We realize we have to pay little heed to supportive "exhortation" individuals as they are most likely going to pick the breed they needed in any case.

In any case, presently, they may feel hesitant to prepare the young dog, feeling that the procedure will be troublesome and tedious. Besides, proprietors may legitimize their carelessness by referring to any of the pack of advantageous reasons recorded previously.

The breed is an individual decision. Pick the kind you like, examine breed-explicit characteristics and issues, and afterward inquire about an ideal approach to raise and prepare your little dog.

In the situation that you select what others think about a pure breed to grow and develop, train your puppy with the goal that he turns into the absolute best pup.

Furthermore, in case you select a kind that a few people think about being hard to raise and prepare, train him, train him, and train him, so he turns into the absolute best model—an exemplary—of that breed.

Despite your possible decision, once you have gotten it, achievement or disappointment is currently entirely in your grasp. Your pup's conduct and disposition presently depend totally on high attention and preparing.

While assessing various breeds, the valid statements are self-evident. What you have to discover are the breed's terrible aspects. You have to explore potential breed-explicit (or line-specific) issues and realize how to manage them.

If you need to discover more about a particular breed, find at any rate six grown-up dogs of the kind you have chosen. Converse with their proprietors finally, yet above all, meet the mutts! Look at and handle them; play with them and work them.

Check whether the mutts welcome being petted by a "more fun you". Will they sit? Do they walk pleasantly on-chain? Is it true that they are calm or uproarious? Are they quiet and composed, or are they hyperactive and rowdy?

Would you be able to look at their ears, eyes, and backside? Would you be able to open their gag? Would you be able to get them to turn over? Are the trainers' homes plants still in excellent condition?

Furthermore, generally significant, do the puppies like individuals and different dogs?

Realize what's in store, since when your eight-week-old little dog returns home, he will grow up with the startling rate. In only few months, your small dog will form into a six-month-old juvenile that has picked up a practically grown-up size, quality, and speed, while simultaneously holding numerous pup imperatives on learning.

Your dog has such a long way to go before he crashes into looming immaturity.

As far as character, conduct, and demeanor, it would be ideal if you know that puppies of a similar breed may show impressive variety.

If you have kid or more than one kid, you most likely value the fantastic scope of demeanors and characters of kids.

CHAPTER THREE

TIME AND PLACE TO GET A PUPPY

BEST TIME TO GET A PUPPY

Besides the undeniable answer—not before you are unprepared—a time to get a puppy is a point at which you have finished your doggy instruction. What's more, when the little dog is ready?

A significant thought is the age of the little dog. Most dogs change homes eventually in their life, ordinarily from the home where they were born to the homes of their new human owners.

The ideal time for a little dog to change homes relies upon numerous factors, including his passionate needs, his significant socialization plan, and the degree of doggy aptitude in every family unit. Leaving the home can be horrendous

If the young dog ventures out from home too soon, he will lose early puppy and pup-mother communications. What's more, since the first weeks in another house are regularly spent in a doggy social vacuum, the little dog may grow up under-socialized toward his sorts.

Then again, the more drawn out the pup remains in his unique home, the more joined he becomes to his doggy family and the harder the inevitable change. Deferred progress additionally defers all important socialization with the new family.

Two months of age has, for quite some time, been acknowledged as the ideal time to procure another little dog.

By about two months, adequate puppy dog socialization has occurred with mother and littermates to hold the dog over until he is mature enough to securely meet and play with different mutts in young dog class and dog parks.

However, the pup is as yet youthfully sufficient to shape a solid bond with the individuals from his new family.

The general degree of doggy aptitude in each house is a crucial thought in deciding if the pup is in an ideal situation remaining longer in his home or leaving for life with his new owners.

It is frequently accepted that raisers are specialists, and proprietors are rank starters, so it speaks well to go the puppy with the reproducer till this would be possible. A scrupulous reproducer usually is better able to mingle, housetrain, and chew toy train the young dog.

At the point when this is valid, it bodes well to get the young dog when he is more grown. (Truth be told, I frequently ask tenderfoot proprietors whether they have considered a socially developed and well-prepared grown-up hound as an option in contrast to a youthful little dog.)

This surmises the reproducer's prevalent mastery. Sadly, similarly, as there are great, average, fledgling, and reckless proprietors, there are additionally fantastic, healthy, tenderfoot, and flighty reproducers.

With the blend of an accomplished proprietor and a not precisely average raiser, the pup would be in an ideal situation moving to his new home as right on time as could be allowed, absolutely by six weeks to about two months at the earliest.

In the case that you believe you are a certified young dog raiser, yet the reproducer won't let you take your puppy home before about two months of age, look somewhere else.

Keep in mind, you are scanning dog for a little dog to live with you, not with the raiser who they were born with. Indeed, you may be in an ideal situation looking somewhere else, since not all reproducers most likely delivers exactly average young dogs.

As a dog reproducer, one of your numerous choices is when to send your young dog's home to their new proprietors. Various components go into choosing that "great" age, and assessments shift on the theme.

Most veterinarians and raisers concur that six weeks-to about two months of age is the prime time for a dog to meet its new family.

In the following, veterinarian and behaviorist Dr. Sally Foote and raiser of working Shetland Sheepdogs Claire Apple says something regarding socialization periods, dread periods, and young dog conduct.

An essential factor in picking when to send a little dog to another house is the socialization period, according to Foote. The socialization time frame in young dogs regularly endures from 6-to-12 weeks of age. During this time, little dogs are learning the standards of their general surroundings.

Foote said that young dogs should enter their new homes at the earliest opportunity during this age range to give them the most apparent chance at adjusting to their original condition.

The first conduct dread period in quite a while additionally happens during this time at around seven to two months, and sending a dog to a new home during this time encourages it to fabricate flexibility to new encounters; Foote said.

Interestingly, Sheltie, a reproducer, likes to keep her little dogs in her home during the socialization time frame. Her young dogs go to their working or game homes at 12 weeks of age.

As such, she said she can control the encounters her pups have during their dread and socialization periods and can start the engagements in preparing the requirement for their future homes.

Socialization of young dogs ought to be done mindfully. Reproducers can mentor their customers on the best way to do this.

Helping proprietors comprehend the requirement for constructive introduction to the world's sights, sounds, individuals, and creatures can go far in keeping pups in their home for a lifetime.

As indicated by Foote, numerous investigations show that proprietors' release of dogs will, in general, happen when the mutts are six to eight months old.

A reproducer's useful help during those many early months can assist proprietors with giving the correct encounters to shape their young dog into a typically sound dog.

Reproducers can provide dogs with a lift the right way with an early presentation to wearing a neckline and rope, bolstering little dogs in independent dishes, and giving a constructive introduction to various surfaces, areas, individuals, and sounds.

Beginning crate training can additionally go far in helping a young dog go to its new home with certainty.

Isabella said she guarantees that her young dogs are well prepared and have necessary compliance skills before they leave. Every one of her young dogs is dealt with separately and offered an introduction to vehicle rides and to the domesticated animals with which they are going to share grounds.

She takes them to visit new areas and new individuals frequently. "I need to have them started on house-preparing; be chain prepared; have come, sit down, and other works began.

Puppies may likewise have been riding in the vehicle a few times each week from about a month on, so no carsickness," Isabella said. "They will have been to town, met various breeds, and numerous individuals."

That introduction to new things and individual consideration are significant if reproducers decide to keep dogs past the age of about two months; Foote said.

Little dogs that stay in the solace of the litter during their dread period may pass up the opportunity to figure out how to adapt to new encounters, just as they conceivably could.

A young dog that is excessively protected during this time could get on edge or frightful around new things and take more time to adjust to unique circumstances.

Another potential concern when keeping litters together for a long time is the distinction of every dog. "Those little dogs are not suited for their very own individual needs," Foote said.

If litters are just worked with as a gathering, a couple of pups will undoubtedly pass up a significant opportunity.

A timid pup in a litter of rowdy puppies might be constrained into circumstances. Or a boisterous little dog in a gathering of calmer ones may not get the degree of incitement it needs.

It's significant that reproducers who keep their small dogs through this period set aside the effort to stay away from potential conduct difficulties to raise sure youthful puppies; Foote said.

Isolating pups from their moms too early, just as weaning too soon, can have undesirable impacts,

Foote said. From three weeks to about a month and a half, little dogs are in an early socialization period, figuring out how to be hounded.

Through their mom and littermates, little dogs start to learn proper play practices. They additionally learn simple drive control and chomp restraint from the input of their fellow kin and mom.

A dog isolated a month and a half after birth may pass up a portion of this early learning. In the case that a dog must return home before seven weeks to about two months of age, Foote suggests it be "guided" by a more seasoned pup or tolerant puppy.

Despite whether a raiser decides to send a pup home at about two months or 12 weeks, unmistakably, what occurs during the weeks between is what makes a difference. This touchy period for socialization shapes a youthful young dog's future as a puppy. As significant as bloodlines, legitimate socialization will give a young dog a head start.

It should be a typically sound accomplice, in the home, show ring, or field.

Dr. Sally Foote is a veterinarian and Universal Relationship of Creature Conduct expert. She likewise is the present head of a Dog Distributing agency. She rehearses at Okaw Veterinary Center in Tuscola.

Isabella is the proprietor of a dog care center in New Jersey. She specifically breeds Shetland Sheepdogs and shows compliance and grouping to all breeds.

THE BEST PLACE TO GET A PUPPY

In the case of choosing your planned little dog from an expert raiser or from a family reproducing a litter for the absolute first time, the criteria are the same.

To start with, search for little dogs raised inside around human friendship and impact. Dodge small dogs brought up in an outside run or pet house.

Keep in mind that you need a dog to share your home, thus search for a pup that has been brought up in a home. Second thing, quest for your forthcoming young dog's present socialization and instruction status.

Notwithstanding breed, rearing, family, and genealogy, if your planned socialization and preparing programs are not well in progress by about two months of age, he is as of now formatively hindered.

A decent reproducer will be incredibly fussy in tolerating planned little dog purchasers. A planned proprietor ought to be similarly meticulous when choosing a raiser.

A forthcoming owner may start to assess a raiser's skill by noticing whether she positions the pups' psychological level and physical wellbeing over their great looks.

Evaluate a few elements: regardless of whether the raiser's grown-up hounds are for the most part human benevolent and well-prepared; whether your planned young dog's folks live to a mature age; and whether your forthcoming little dog is as of now well-mingled and well-prepared.

Amicable puppies are self-obvious when you meet them, thus meet whatever a number of your planned little dog's family members as would be prudent.

Benevolent mutts are living verification of proper socialization by a decent reproducer.

Be careful the reproducer is just there to give you young dogs. Initially, a great raiser will set aside the effort to perceive how you coexist with grown-up hounds before letting you any place close to the little dogs.

A decent raiser wouldn't let you leave with a pup in the case that you did not in any way have the slightest idea how to deal with a grown-up hound, which your pup will be in only a couple of months.

Second, you need to assess; however, how many grown-up hounds as could be allowed from your planned pup's family before you let a litter of very adorable young dogs win your love.

If all the grown-up hounds are human amicable and polite, it is a decent to say that you have found an outstanding reproducer.

The absolute best pointer of general wellbeing, exemplary conduct, and disposition is the vague future of a pet house line.

Verify that your planned young dog's folks, grandparents, great grandparents, and different relations are as yet alive and stable or that they passed on at a mature age.

Reliable raisers will have phone numbers promptly accessible for past little dog purchasers and the reproducers of different mutts in your planned dog's family.

In the case that the reproducer isn't anxious to share data concerning the future and the rate of breed-explicit sicknesses, look somewhere else. You will, in the long run, discover a reproducer who will oblige your interests.

Before you open your heart to a youthful little dog, you need to be able to give a good level of probability that you two will spend a long and stable coexistence.

Also, seemingly perpetual dogs publicize great demeanor and preparing since hounds with conduct and personality issues, for the most part, have short futures.

Moreover, a two-year-old (or more seasoned) grown-up dog's propensities, habits, and personality are now entrenched, for better or in negative ways.

Qualities and inclinations may change after some time, yet contrasted and the social adaptability of young dogs, a more seasoned dog's great propensities are as impervious to change as their negative behavior patterns.

Like this, it is conceivable to test drive various grown-up cover hounds and select one liberated from issues and one with a built-up character just as you would prefer.

Embracing a grown-up hound from an animal asylum or salvage association can be a great option in contrast to raising a young dog. Some safe house and salvage hounds are well-prepared and essentially need a home.

Others have a couple of conduct issues and require therapeutic young dog training in adulthood. A few dogs are thoroughbred; most are blended breeds. The way to finding a decent haven or salvage hound is determination, choice, and choice! Set aside a lot of effort to test drive each planned applicant.

Each dog is one of a kind.

If, despite everything, you have your heart set on raising and preparing a little dog, do ensure you teach yourself beforehand.

Search for a young dog after you have figured out how to build and make one. Keep in mind. It takes just half a month to make a generally impeccable young dog.

In the situation that it is not too much trouble enquire from yourself, "Where do despised hounds originate from?"

All asylum hounds were once immaculate little dogs that were deserted or gave up because they created irritating conduct, preparing, and personality issues, mainly because their proprietors didn't have the foggiest idea how to prepare them.

The grouping of occasions is unsurprising: an excessive amount of the first opportunity and too little supervision and training.

In the proprietor's endeavor to deal with these regular and predictable issues, the young dog is consigned outside, where he rapidly becomes de-mingled and creates other irritating propensities, for example, yapping, burrowing, and getting away.

In the wake of going through for quite a while in social disconnection, the little dog is so energized when asked inside that he eagerly goes around, barks, and bounces up to welcome his seemingly deceased human mates.

Before long, the excessively loud little dog is never again permitted inside. He may be caught by creature control after he escapes from isolation, or neighbors grumble about his over the top barking.

And he is kept to the carport or storm cellar—typically just a transitory measure before the now undesirable pre-adult dog is given up or relinquished. What's more, he is scarcely a half year old.

All conduct, demeanor, and preparing issues are so completely unsurprising, thus effectively preventable. Indeed, even most existing matters might be settled decently effectively. Instruction is the key.

Regardless of whether you choose to get a pup or receive a grown-up hound if you don't mind getting your young dog or adult dog.

There are a vast number of undesirable mutts. Millions are euthanized every year; kindly don't add to the numbers.

CHAPTER FOUR

Puppy Classes

A compelling degree of socialization is appropriate in the creation of a legitimate, keen, and fit puppy.

Weakness, furious and disagreeableness to individuals is related to the degrees of preparing and socialization.

Class (PC) was initially created to prepare pups enough to avoid conduct issues, and it changes from the preparation providing for grown-up hounds on submission.

The Pup class is a socialization school where pups start to figure out how to live with individuals and different puppies at such a young age. The pup's proprietor casually teaches direction, preparing, and mindful puppy possession.

As indicated by different investigations, most little dogs show positive and agreeable practices after the young dog socialization class.

A decent number of analysts have advanced in logically building up the impacts of Pup class preparing. This implies the enlistment of little dogs in a dog class can assume extremely significant jobs in the conduct advancement of pups.

Dog class additionally includes central submission preparing and socialization with individuals and other infant hounds. In Japan, for example, fundamental submission class for immature/grown-up hounds is better known than dog class.

We guess that the PC and the adult class (air conditioning) effectively affect puppy conduct, especially as far as socialization. In this manner, a preliminary young dog instructional meeting called "pup party" (PP) is at present being polished in Japan. It has been seen that members were enrolled more effectively for PP than PC.

In this investigation, we contrasted conducted consequences for mutts and four unique sorts of instructional course experience: PC, PP, Air conditioning, and NC (no class).

For the assessment of puppy practices, a conducted test was performed at the proprietor's home to examine the dog's social conduct towards individuals, reaction to being taking care of and directions of the proprietor or outsiders, response to an improvement and response to being partitioned.

Also, the Puppy Conduct Evaluation and Exploration Survey (C-BARQ) [20] was utilized to distinguish any hostility in the dog's day by day lead that probably won't be adequately recognized by the social test.

CHAPTER FIVE

UNDERSTANDING YOUR PUPPY

By the time you bring your new young dog home, say at about two months of age, she should as of now be acclimated with an indoor household condition (particularly one with commotions) and well-mingled with people.

So also, housetraining, chew toy-preparing, and coaching in fundamental habits ought to be well in progress.

If not, your imminent little dog's social and mental improvement is as of now seriously in danger, and tragically, you will play make up for lost time for a mind-blowing remainder. Your young dog will require medicinal socialization and preparing for quite a while to come.

Be very sure that your planned young dog has been brought inside up in close contact with individuals who have given good time to instructing het.

In the situation that a dog is required to live in a family with individuals, she needs to have been brought up in a family with individuals.

Your dog should be set up for the fuss of ordinary local living: the commotion of the vacuum cleaner, pots and container dropping in the kitchen, football match causing shouting to the TV, kids/babies crying, and grown-ups contending.

Presentation to such improvements while her eyes and ears are as yet getting more accustomed, (with her obscured vision and suppressed hearing) to bit by bit become familiar with sights and sounds that though may terrify her when more intense.

There isn't any point in picking a pup that has been brought up in the relative social disengagement of a lawn, storm cellar, animal dwelling place, carport, or pet house, where there is only little chance for communication with individuals and where a dog has gotten acclimated with being in her living zone and barking a great deal. Pups brought up in physical confinement, and fractional social segregation are not arranged for family unit living, and they are positively not set up for experiences with kids or men.

Backyard and pet hotel raised little dogs are not pet-quality dogs; they are animals comparable to veal calves and battery hens. Look somewhere else! Search for litters brought up inside.

If you need a partner dog to share your home, she needs to be trained in a home, not a pen.

Your imminent little dog should feel altogether quiet being taken care of by outsiders—you and your family. The young dog ought to be wholly desensitized to sounds before he is a month old.

Similarly, his housetraining system ought to be well in progress, his preferred toy ought to be a chew toy (loaded down with pup chow), and he ought to joyfully and energetically come, pursue, sit, rests, and turn over when mentioned.

In the case that these are not real, either your little dog is a moderate learner, or he has had a poor educator. In either case, look somewhere else.

An essential element of dog cultivation is customary (a few times each day) dealing with, gentling, and quieting by a wide assortment of individuals, particularly kids, men, and outsiders.

These activities are particularly significant during the early weeks and particularly with those breeds that are famously precarious when dealt with by outsiders—that is, a few Asian breeds, in addition to any grouping, working, and terrier breeds.

The second most significant quality in any dog is that he appreciates connecting with individuals, and explicitly that he enjoys being dealt with by all individuals, particularly youngsters, men, and outsiders.

Early socialization effectively averts genuine growing-up issues.

If it would be easy to recall, the absolute significant quality for a dog is to create a chomp hindrance and a delicate mouth during puppyhood.

Dealing with it and Gentling

If you need a cuddly grown-up hound, he needs to have been snuggled, usually like a dog. Positively, neonatal puppies are entirely delicate and powerless critters; they can scarcely walk and they have various tactile requirements.

However, regardless they should be mingled. Newborn puppies are incredibly sensitive and naïve. And this is the absolute best time to familiarize them with being dealt with.

Neonatal pups may not see or hear quite well. However, they can smell and feel. Neonatal and early young dog socialization, being of foremost significance, must be done tenderly and cautiously.

Sound Sensitivity

Presentation to an assortment of sounds ought to initiate a long time before the eyes and ears are completely opened, particularly with sound-sensitive mutts, for example, crowding and acquiescence breeds.

It is very typical for little dogs to respond to clamors. What you are attempting to assess is the degree of each puppy's response and the little dog's bob back time.

For instance, we anticipate that a young dog should respond to an abrupt and startling noisy clamor; however, we don't expect that he should turn out badly.

Judge whether the pup meets or blows up to sounds, and time to what extent it adopts for the little dog to strategy and take a nourishment treat (the bob back time).

Anticipate immensely short skip-back occasions from bully breeds, and short ricochet-backs from working puppies and terriers, which are set up for longer bob-back occasions from toys and crowding kinds.

Notwithstanding a dog's breed or type, be that as it may, amazingly extensive bounce back times are on the whole evidence of lacking socialization.

Except if effectively restored, such little dogs may turn out to be incredibly receptive and hard to live with when they grow up.

- Ask the raiser about the degree of the litter's presentation to residential clamor. Are the dogs being raised inside?
- Specifically, ask the raiser whether the little dogs have been presented to boisterous and surprising commotions, for example, grown-

ups yelling, kids crying, TV (male voices yelling and shouting on ESPN), radio, and music (Country, Rock, and Classical—possibly Tchaikovsky's 1812 Overture).

- Evaluate the young dogs' reaction to an assortment of clamors: individuals talking, chuckling, crying, and yelling, a whistle, a murmur, or a solitary hand applaud.

Family unit Etiquette

Get some information about the litter's progressing errorless housetraining and chew toy-repairing program. Attempt to watch the litter for around two hours and focus on what every pup bites and where every little dog disposes off.

If the young dogs have no open bin and the whole little dog zone has been littered with sheets of paper, the pups will have built up a solid inclination for going on paper and will require particular housetraining in their new home.

Besides, if there is a bin and the whole territory has been covered with straw or destroyed paper, the young dogs will have learned that they may take it out from anyplace, which is the thing that they will do in your home.

The more extended the young dog has been brought up in the aforementioned conditions, the more troublesome she will be to housetrain.

- Check for the utilization of a few non-usable (for example, Biscuit Balls, or disinfected bones) loaded down with kibble.
- Check for the usage of a doggy latrine in the little dogs' living zone. Looking at what number of heaps and puddles are in the poo-place versus on the floor will offer a decent sign of where the little dog will wipe out when she goes to your home.

Fundamental Manners

Ask about the litter's progressing compliance preparing program and request that the reproducer show the pups' essential submission abilities, for instance, to come, sit, rest, and turn over.

- Evaluate every young dog's reaction to your bait/reward, preparing endeavors utilizing bits of kibble and a Kong as baits and rewards.

Individual Preference

While picking the dog, it is critical to such an extent that all relatives concur. You need to choose the young dog all of you like best, and you need to select a little dog who every one of you loves.

Plunk down discreetly as a family and see which young dogs reach first and which ones remain around the longest.

For a considerable length of time, it was fanatically expressed that pups that drew closer immediately bounced up, and bit your hands were inadmissible as pets since they were forceful and hard to prepare. Despite what might be expected, these are ordinary and well-mingled.

With some extremely fundamental preparing to divert the little dog's incredible richness, you'll have the quickest reviews, and the snappiest sits in pup class.

Additionally, young dog gnawing is both typical and utterly vital. Truth be told, the more dogs nibble as little dogs, the milder and more secure their jaws in adulthood.

I would be increasingly worried about little dogs that were delayed to approach or stayed sequestered from everything. It is, ultimately, and unusual for a well-mingled six to eight week-old little dog to be bashful when moving towards individuals.

In the situation that the little dog acts modest or frightened, at that point doubtlessly, he has not been adequately mingled. Look somewhere else.

Assuming, you genuinely have your heart set on taking a bashful dog, possibly do as such if every relative can urge the puppy to approach and take a nourishment treat.

To restore this little dog's trend of not being comfortable around visitors, you'll surely have a difficult, but not impossible task ahead during the following a month.

Be careful with reproducers who need to choose for you whether to raise your puppy for compliance or have him fixed. Keep in mind; the young dog is coming to live with you.

Raising the puppy is your duty, and choices concerning his show vocation and conceptive status are yours to make.

You can appreciate various magnificent exercises with your puppy, including focused, rally, and free-form dutifulness, dexterity, trucking, fly ball, Frisbee, K9 Games, search and salvage, sledding, following, and obviously, hound strolls and outings to the dog leave.

It's altogether your decision; however, please train your young dog. Every year, a great number of little dogs and grown-up hounds are euthanized (executed) in creature covers.

It's mostly not reasonable for dogs, and it isn't feasible for creature cherishing cover work force. Kindly don't add to the numbers. Kindly fix your young dog.

CHAPTER SIX

Adjustment Time

(Dos and Don'ts)

The Adjustment Period

Give your new puppy time to change following his/her new home. It takes hounds, at any go, a month to feel great and to show their actual character.

It can take hounds as long as THREE months to get accustomed and agreeable in another condition.

Directly from the very first moment, it is critical to set house rules for your dog, for example, "no jumping on the furnishings," "no bouncing on individuals," "no asking for individual's nourishment." Mutts need rules, and it is dependent upon you to set the principles up! Be thoughtful, delicate, and persistent. Established house rules for your new puppy right from the beginning, so he/she recognizes what's in store.

Try not to indulge and child your hound since you feel for him/her. Not all house hounds were mishandled and disregarded.

Regardless of whether they were, pampering them brings about more harm than good. Indulging or petting a terrified or snarling hound lauds the conduct the dog appears right then and there - dread and additional snarling and hostility.

Your new dog will be apprehensive, setting off to another home. Be patient and kind. Pursue the guides in this chapter to help make bringing your new dog home a fruitful as well as a positive experience for the new pup and you.

Before You Take the Dog Home
1. Find a neighborhood coach who offers classes in your general vicinity. You can check for a coach on the Association for Pet Dog Trainers site (E.g. Apdt) Talk with the mentor about to what extent you ought to have the dog before you start classes.

See a couple of classes to check whether you like the coach and his/her style.

2."Dog verify" your home and any territory outside where the puppy will be BEFORE the dog shows up. The viable primary approach to do this is to get down on your hands and knees to perceive what you can see from the dog's point of view. In the case that you don't need it a bit, move it. NOW, before the dog shows up.

3. Parts of the home where the dog isn't wanted ought to be gated, or some route closed off BEFORE the puppy shows up.

4. Withhold nourishment and water until he starts to unwind. Your new puppy will be apprehensive and energized when he first returns home.

Anxious puppies tend to drink a lot of water rapidly, making them hurl it. It is smarter to offer a couple of broke/chipped ice solid shapes rather than water until your new puppy appears to be at ease.

5. Have a case set up and prepared for the puppy. You have to utilize a case at whatever point the puppy can't be directed. If you don't use a box, you could return home to pulverization and house dirtying. If that occurs, it isn't the dog's flaw. It is your deficiency for not crating the dog. The carton will likewise assist you with housebreaking your new puppy.

Fundamental Suggestions for When You First Arrive Home

1. If you have different mutts, go with them when you show up. If you have a cat, it also ought to be in the house.

2. Leash walk your new puppy outside for in any event 10-15 minutes or until he alleviates himself.

Continuously keep your new pet on-chain, in a fenced surrounding. Give him the "lay of the land" by sniffing and getting familiar with every one of the scents related to your yard.

3. New human presentations ought to be made each in turn; ideally, on the rope for additional control should it be required. Let the dog step up and welcome the new individual.

Try not to let individuals approach the dog and power themselves on the puppy. This is what to do:

Give each individual some beautiful treats. You need the puppy's early introduction of everybody in the family.

Keep everything serene and as quiet as could be allowed. Let the dog approach every relative who consequently offers a treat without attempting to contact the puppy!

In the case that the dog reacts well or returns for another gift, it's alright to begin stroking UNDER the jawline.

For hounds that show kind of uncertain attitude, present every relative individually with the dog in a sitting situation, on a rope.

Every individual should hurl the dog a treat, say a "welcome" in the most delightful voice conceivable, and afterward retreat from the puppy giving the dog an agreeable space to take the gift.

Rehash this until the dog is loose and friendly. NEVER power the dog to meet another individual or another puppy except if the dog is free and pleasant.

4. Take your signals from your new dog. How agreeable does he show up with the entirety of this additional consideration? Numerous dogs are good hams and love to be inundated by individuals.

Different dogs might be a bit overpowered with their unique circumstances. Sound judgment should control the day.

5. After presentations and the dog is agreeable, drop the rope (leave it on the puppy) and let the hound investigate the zone and approach relatives on the off chance that he wishes.

Each time he moves toward an individual, he gets another treat and possibly petted if the dog seems agreeable and looks for contact. The key here is to make the "initial introductions" of his new home and new "pack mates" as tranquil and remunerating as could be expected under the circumstances.

Point of confinement for underlying welcome session with everybody present should be close to 15 minutes at that point change the situation, for example, a stroll outside. You might need to arrange a rehash of the main session later in the day.

New Dog Meets Old Dog

The gathering between dogs may have gone brilliantly on the unbiased turf of the asylum. On home turf, the response from either of the two mutts might be extraordinary. This distinction is because you are presently bringing another puppy into your present dog's home turf.

1. Meeting outside (ideally in a fenced yard) can be less compromising for puppy presentations. Set things up, so this should be possible.

2. Both puppies must be on-chain and wearing secure clasp collars, preparing collars, or Gentle Leaders for better control during the presentations.

3. Introduce each puppy each in turn. Try not to constrain an encounter! Allow them to move toward one another.

4. If there is any indication of a threatening vibe, remind the antagonistic puppy in a firm tone, "Be Nice." Keep the weight OFF the rope. You should act as the owner-not stressed.

You are in charge and should know about their non-verbal communication. Try not to be concerned if they don't warm up to one another right away. Give consolation for ethical conduct. (Great - be pleasant.)

As hard as it might be, make an effort not to be anxious yourself, or you will broadcast it to the dogs.

Your dog may feel you need to be protected from the new puppy or even vice Versa.

In the situation that they take part in a battle, don't attempt to pull them separated with the rope if the chains have gotten trapped. In many cases, the strings become wrapped, and all you end up doing is compelling them closer together.

If that occurs, drop either of the rope so the dogs can move away from one another. At that point, get the chains once more. The significance of doing presentations in a fenced territory gets self-evident.

If you need to drop the rope, neither one of the dogs can get away from the yard.

5. As each dog gets settled with the other, you can cut the chains (if in a fenced domain). Keep the rope on so you can all the more effectively snatch one rapidly if necessary.

6. As the puppies come inside, you may notice this more; progressively getting close to home space will cause a quarrel or two, so you may, in any case, need to leave the rope on for fast control.

7. Do not sustain the dogs directly beside one another. A few mutts are incredibly defensive of their nourishment.

One of the puppies may want to secure his food, and a battle can result. Feed them separated, so neither wants to watch the nourishment bowl.

Acquainting Your New Dog with Your Cat

1. You will require an increasingly controlled condition to familiarize your new dog with your feline. Try not to present them the moment you return home.

If you were told the dog coexists with felines, it doesn't mean your feline and the new puppy will immediately become companions.

It requires some investment, and you must guard them two. Try not to push the association. Give them time.

2. Keep your dog on the rope and have him meet the feline where the feline can't flee and cover-up.

3. It is perfect to put either the puppy or the cat into a container and let them meet unobtrusively - giving every nourishment treats for quietness and tranquility.

4. Don't ever release your dog around your cat until you feel entirely right about their cooperation. Until you are confident, don't leave the puppy and cat solo.

Most dogs possibly may begin to pursue the cat in a situation that it runs, yet sometimes, a more grounded prey drive may make the puppy increasingly forceful, and the cat can be harmed or even rendered dead.

What to do and what not in the 1st to 3rd Month of Adjustment Period

1. DO NOT disregard your new puppy or leave under the supervision of any children, paying little mind to age, whenever, in any way, shape or form.

If this is done, you are setting the puppy up for disappointment, also to likely harm a kid. Right or wrong, the owner is ALWAYS to blame when an occurrence happens with a youngster.

2. Introduce the dog to the case and utilize the carton! You have to use a box at whatever point the puppy can't be directed. In the situation that you don't use a container, you could get back home to devastation and house dirtying.

In a condition that such occurs, it isn't the dog's deficiency. It is your shortcoming for not crating the dog. The carton will likewise assist you with housebreaking your new puppy.

Also, your puppy will require his very own position where he/she can rest, be sheltered, and unwind.

3. for the initial 30 days, don't uncover your new dog to any unpleasant occasions, for example, parties,

substantial family get-togethers, or outings to other loved ones.

4. For the initial two weeks, watch the puppy intently and TAKE NOTES of odd practices or negative responses to items and circumstances. Instances of such conduct incorporate, yet are not constrained to:

A .growling or yelping at a specific relative

B. resource guarding conduct (nourishment or toys)

C. hyperactivity

D. barking/dangerous conduct when taken off alone

E. staying alone inside

CHAPTER SEVEN

BONDING WITH YOUR DOG AND EXPANDING YOUR DOGS INTELLIGENCE

Your puppy newcomer is only tingling to learn family unit habits. She needs to, it would be ideal if you bond with her and show her, yet she needs to figure out how things are.

Before the youthful little dog can be trusted to have full run in the house, someone must instruct the house rules. There's no point keeping house governs a mystery.

Someone needs to tell the little dog. What's more, that someone is you. Something else, your young dog will let her creative mind go crazy as she continues looking for word related solutions to take a break. Without a firm establishing in puppy's social decorum, your young dog will be left to mingle in her decision of toys and toilets.

The puppy will definitely wipe out in storerooms and on rugs, and your love seats and mores will be seen as insignificant toys for obliteration. Each error is a potential fiasco, since it breeds a lot more to come.

In the case that your little dog is permitted to make "botches", negative behavior patterns will immediately turn into business as usual, making it essential to bring an end to unfortunate propensities before showing great ones.

Start by showing your young dog great propensities from the entire first day she gets back home.

Keep in mind; significant tendencies are similarly as difficult to get out from under as negative behavior patterns. Generally squeezing, your young dog's living quarters should be structured so that housetraining and chew toy training are errorless.

Errorless Housetraining and Chew toy-Training

Effective local doggy instruction includes showing your young dog to prepare herself through control.

This anticipates botches and builds up great propensities from the start. At the point when you are physically or rationally missing, limit your pup to keep her out of fiendishness and to assist her with figuring out acceptable behavior correctly.

The more you keep your pup to her Doggy Den and Puppy Playroom during her initial weeks at home, the more opportunity she will get as a grown-up hound for a fantastic member. The more intently you stick to the accompanying puppy confinement program, the sooner your little dog will be housetrained, and chew toy prepared.

Furthermore, as an additional advantage, your young dog will figure out how to settle down rapidly, discreetly, smoothly, and cheerfully.

At the point when you Are Not at Home

Keep your little dog restricted to a genuinely small young dog den and away from places like, the kitchen, restroom, or utility room.

You can likewise utilize an activity pen to cordon off a little segment of a place. This is your pup's long haul imprisonment zone. It ought to include:

1. A Comfortable Bed

2. A Water Bowl with crisp water

3. Six Hollow Chew toys (loaded down with hound nourishment)

4. A Doggy Toilet in the most distant corner from her bed. Obviously, your young dog will want to bark, bite, and dispose of over the day. Thus she should be left someplace she can fulfill her needs without creating any harm or disturbance.

Your young dog will most likely wipe out beyond what many would consider possible from her resting quarters—in her doggy latrine.

By expelling every single chewable thing from the pup playpen—except for empty chew toys loaded down with kibble—you will make biting chew toys your pup's preferred propensity, a high one indeed!

Long haul repression enables your little dog to instruct herself to utilize a fitting dogs would to need to bite proper chew toys, and to settle down unobtrusively.

At the point when you are at Home

Appreciate short play and instructional meetings hourly. If you can't give full consideration to your little dog's every second, play with your small dog in his Puppy Playpen, where a reasonable latrine and toys are accessible.

Or, on the other hand, for times of no longer than an hour at once, bind your little dog to his Doggy Den (transient close constrainment zone, for example, a compact puppy carton). Then discharge your little dog and take him to his doggy box.

Your young dog's momentary constrained territory should incorporate an agreeable bed, and a lot of empty chew toys (loaded down with hound nourishment).

It is a lot simpler to watch your puppy if he is settled down in a secluded spot. Possibly you may move the box with the goal that your young dog is in a similar room as you, or you might need to bind your little dog to an alternate space to begin setting him up for times when he will be disregarded at home.

In a case that you don't care for keeping your young dog to a puppy container, you may attach the rope to your belt and have the little dog settle down at your feet.

Or then again, you may connect the line to an eye-snare in the baseboard alongside your dog's bed, container, or tangle. To avert the chew toys from turning distant, likewise, attach them to the eye-snare.

Train Your Puppy to Train Himself

Housetraining and chew toy-preparing will be snappy and straightforward in the case that you hold fast to the young dog's repression plan above, which keeps the pup from committing errors and prompts the puppy to show family unit decorum.

In a case that you do what's different from the program, you will probably encounter issues. Except if you appreciate problems, you should blame yourself for any mix-ups you enable your dog to make.

Errorless Housetraining

House soiling is a spatial issue, including consummately typical, regular, and fundamental puppy practices (peeing and crapping) acted in awkward spots.

Housetraining is rapidly and effectively achieved by applauding your little dog and offering a nourishment treat when she makes an outstanding feat.

When your small dog understands that her eliminatory items, that dung and pee might be traded out for delectable treats—your puppy will noise to dispose of in the proper spot, since ruining the house doesn't bring incidental comparative advantages.

House soiling is additionally a practical issue: either the little dog is in an inappropriate spot at the correct time (limited inside with full bladder and guts), or the young dog is in the suitable place at an inopportune time (outside or on a walk, however with void bladder and entrails).

Timing is the embodiment of fruitful housetraining. Without a doubt, productive and powerful housetraining relies on the proprietor having the option to anticipate when the little dog needs to dispense with so she might be coordinated to a fitting latrine zone and more than satisfactorily rewarded for making the best choice in the perfect spot at the ideal time.

For the most part, young dogs pee generally after awakening from a snooze and generally poo within few minutes after that.

Be that as it may, who has the opportunity to stay nearby to trust that young dog will wake up and pee and crap? Instead, it's a superior intends to awaken the young dog yourself when you are prepared, and all is good and well

Momentary repression offers a helpful way to anticipate when your little dog needs to assuage herself precisely.

Keeping a puppy to a bit of region emphatically hinders her from peeing or pooping since she wouldn't like to soil her dozing zone. Subsequently, the young dog is almost certain to need to wipe out following being discharged from control.

In a situation that errorless housetraining is so natural, for what reason do such a significant number of dog proprietors experience issues?

Here are some essential inquiries and answers that help make errorless housetraining work.

Why keep the puppy to his doggy cave? Why not his den? Transient close caging enables you to foresee when your young dog needs to go with the goal that you might be there to guide him to the suitable spot and prize him for making the best choice in the appropriate place at the correct time.

During the hour-extensive stretches of close control, as your little dog lies doggo in marvelous rest, his bladder and guts are gradually topping off.

At whatever point the large hand arrives at twelve and you obediently discharge the little dog to hurry to his indoor latrine or terrace doggy box to alleviate himself, your young dog is probably going to dispose of right now.

Knowing when your pup needs to go enables you to pick the spot and, above all, to reward your little dog liberally for utilizing it. Compensating your small dog for using his latrine is the key to effective housetraining.

If then again the little dog were left in his den, he would in all probability utilize his indoor and yet would not be rewarded for doing as such. Consider the possibility that your pup doesn't care about going in his container.

Before keeping your pup to his container (doggy sanctum), you first need to instruct him to cherish the carton and to take to restrictions.

This is so natural to do. Stuff a few empty chew toys with kibble and the occasional treat. Let your young dog sniff the stuffed chew toys and afterward place them in the box and close the entryway with your little dog outwards.

Typically there's nothing more needed than a couple of moments for your young dog to implore you to open the entryway and let him inside.

In a matter of seconds, by any means, your little dog will be joyfully engrossed with his chew toys.

When leaving the young dog in his long haul constrainment zone, attach the stuffed chew toys within the case and leave the box entryway open.

Subsequently, the dog can pick whether he needs to investigate the little territory or rests on his bed in his box, attempt to remove the kibble, and treats from his chew toys.

Mostly, the stuffed chew toys are restricted to the carton, and the little dog is given the alternative of coming or going voluntarily. Most pups decide to rest serenely inside the box with stuffed chew toys. This procedure works particularly well if your little dog isn't kibble nourished from a bowl, however just from chew toys or by hand.

To utilize this technique, every morning measure out the little dog's day by day apportion of nourishment into a sack to abstain from overloading.

Transient repression, regardless of whether to a box or secure, is a transitory preparing measure to assist you with showing your dog where to take out and what to bite. A puppy container is the best housetraining instrument to help you precisely foresee when your dog wishes to ease herself and is the best preparing apparatus to assist you with teaching your little dog to turn into a "chewtoyaholic".

When your young dog has figured out how to dispense in suitable regions and to bite just decently, she should be fine in the house not needing anyone to nurse her around.

You will most likely discover nonetheless, that after only a couple of days, your little dog figures out how to adore her case and will herself rest inside. Your little dog's one of a kind sanctum is a tranquil, agreeable, and an extraordinary doggy place.

Why not leave the young dog outside until he is housetrained? Who is going to housetrain your little dog outside—the neighbors? You, most definitely.

In a situation that the puppy is left outside unattended, he will end up being an aimless eliminator. Fundamentally, your little dog will figure out how to go anyplace he needs, at whatever point he needs, and he will probably do the equivalent at whatever point you let him inside.

Little dogs left outside and solo for extensive period may later on become housetrained. Additionally, they will, in general, become unpredictable barkers, chewers, diggers, and idealists, and they might be all the more effectively taken. Outside little dogs additionally become so energized on the couple of events they are welcomed inside that, in the long run, they are never again permitted inside.

Pups have a 45-minute bladder limit at three weeks of age, a 75-minute limit at about two months, an hour and a half limit at twelve weeks, and a two-hour limit at 18 weeks.

Discharging your young dog consistently offers you an hourly chance to compensate your dog for utilizing an assigned latrine region. You don't need to do this exactly every hour, except it is a lot simpler to make sure to do so every hour on the hour.

If you take as much time as is needed getting your pup to his doggy bathroom, you may find that he pees or craps on the way.

Rushing your dog will shake his entrails and bladder with the aim that he truly needs to go the minute you let him stop and sniff his box territory.

Why not just put the little dog outside? Wouldn't he be able to do it all alone? He can. In any case, the general purpose of anticipating when your small dog needs to ease himself is so you can give show him where and offer merited applause and a gift too if available.

Therefore your young dog will realize where you might want him to go. Additionally, in a situation that you see your little dog dispose of, you know that he is vacant; you may then permit your empty young dog to roam around the house for some time before returning him to his cave.

Why train the little dog to attack? Doesn't he realize he needs to take action? By educating your dog to kill already, and by remunerating him for wiping out a short time later, you will show your little dog to take move on an order.

Wiping out on prompt is a help when you are going with your puppy and in other time-obliged circumstances. Request that your little dog "Pick up the pace".

"Do your thing", "Go Pee and Poop," or utilize some other socially worthy, metaphorical eliminatory order.

After that, generally, a youthful little dog will pee within 30 seconds of being discharged from momentary repression.

However, it might take a couple of minutes for him to poop. It is positively beneficial to allow for your little dog three minutes to finish his business.

Imagine a scenario in which the young dog doesn't go.

Your dog will be bound to dispense of in the case that you stop and let him hover around you on the rope. In a situation that your little dog doesn't dispose of inside the dispensed time, no big deal!

Just pop the little dog back in his carton and attempt again in about 30 minutes. Rehash the procedure again and again until he eliminates it. In the end, your pup will take out outside, and it may bring a will to compensate him.

Along these lines, on ensuing hourly excursions to his restroom, your young dog will probably dispense with immediately.

Why acclaim the little dog?

It is far better to make apparent your feelings while adulating your young dog for hitting the nail on the head, than while blaming the poor little dog for missing the point.

So truly acclaim that little dog: "Goooooooooood Puppy!" Housetraining is no time for downplayed expressions of gratitude. Try not to be humiliated about adulating your young dog. Humiliated dog proprietors, as a rule, end up with house soiling issues. Truly reward your young dog. Tell your young dog that he has done a really cool and beautiful thing!

Why offer treats? Isn't lauding an enough?

In a word, no! The average individual can't viably commend doomed lettuce. Also, explicitly, numerous proprietors—particularly men—appear to be unequipped for convincingly complimenting their young dogs.

This way, it would undoubtedly be smart thinking to give the puppy a nourishment treat or two (or three) for his exertion isn't needed. The pup notices that each time she pees or craps outdoors, you always offering me a treat. When it's done on the couch, she never get good treatments.

Till your pup has a perception of "I can hardly wait for my proprietor to return home so I can go out in the yard and cash in my pee and dung for nourishment treats!"

Why freeze-dried liver?

Housetraining is one of those occasions when you need to haul out the entirety of the stops. Trust me: When it comes to housetraining, utilize the Ferrari of dog treats—freeze-dried liver.

Do we genuinely need to give three liver treats when the dog pees or poos? Isn't this a small piece?

Yes and no. Unquestionably you don't need to give your little dog precisely three treats. In any case, it's a smart thing: If I propose that individuals offer a gift each time their little dog takes out expeditiously in the perfect spot, they once in a while adhere to guidelines.

At whatever point I advise individuals to give three treats, in any case, they will meticulously tally out the gifts to provide for their dog.

This is what I am attempting to state: Handsome commendations and prize your little dog each time he utilizes an assigned canzone.

Why play with the little dog inside?

In the case that you reward your little dog for utilizing his doggy restroom, you will realize he is fulfilled. What better moment to chuckle with or train your dog inside without confronting the danger of a chaotic misstep.

Why get a little dog except if you need to go through some quality time with him?

Why try to take a more seasoned dog outside for a walk when he's unfilled?

Numerous individuals fall into the snare of taking their little dog outside or strolling him so he may dispose of, and when he does, they bring him inside.

Usually, all that's needed is a few preliminaries before the dog learns, "At whatever point my pee or defecation hits the ground, my walk closes!"

Consequently, the little dog gets hesitant to dispose of outside, and thus when brought home after an extended shaking play or walk, he is in desperate need to alleviate himself, which he does.

99

It is a vastly improved arrangement to applaud your little dog for utilizing his doggy latrine and afterward go with him for a stroll as a compensation for taking out.

Acclaim the little dog and offer liver treats when he does: "Great puppy, we should go walkies!" Clean up and discard the dung in your very own refuse can, and afterward proceed to appreciate a poopless stroll with your dog.

After only a couple of days with a basic "no crap—no walk" rule, you'll see you have the speediest urinator and defecator around.

What is advisable for me to do if I've done all the above mentioned and I notice the pup falling in an error?

You didn't adhere to the directions above. Who permitted the pee and-dung filled young dog to have unfenced access to your home?

You! Should you ever denounce or rebuff your little dog when you notice him in the demonstration, all he will learn is to dispose of stealthily—that is, never again in your dishonest nearness.

In this way, you will have made an owner absent house soiling issue. In a situation that you ever get your little dog in the act of committing an error that was your issue, at the most, you can rapidly, delicately, yet earnestly implore your puppy, "Outside, outside, outside!"

The tone and direness of your voice convey that you need your pup to accomplish something instantly, and the importance of the words train the young dog.

Your reaction will have a limited impact on the present error, yet it counteracts future mix-ups.

Never blame your puppy in a way that is demeaning. Vague reprove make more issues (proprietor missing misconduct) just as startling the little dog and disintegrating the pup proprietor relationship.

Your young dog is certainly not an "awful little dog." despite what might be expected, your pup is a decent pup that has been compelled to act up because his proprietor proved unable, or would not, adhere to basic directions.

The Doggy Toilet

For the best doggy latrine, prepare a litter box or spread a bit of old flooring with what will be the puppy's possible can material.

For instance, for rustic and rural puppies who will, in the long run, be instructed to diminish themselves outside on earth or grass, set out a move of turf.

For urban pups who will, in the long term be notified to get rid of curbside, set out two or three beautiful solid tiles. Your puppy will before long, build up a robust characteristic inclination for killing on comparable open-air surfaces at whatever point he can.

If you have a terrace hound can region, notwithstanding the indoor den restroom, take your little dog to his open-air can in the yard at whatever point you discharge him from his doggy cave.

If you live in a loft and don't have a yard, train your dog to utilize his indoor can until he is mature enough to wander outside at a quarter of a year of age.

Preparing Your Dog to Use an Outdoor Toilet

For the initial weeks, take your little dog outside on-rope. Rush to his latrine zone and afterward stop to enable the pup to hover (as he would ordinarily do before dispensing with).

Prize your puppy each time he "goes" in the assigned spot; In a case that you have an all-round fenced yard, you may later take your young dog outside off-chain and let him pick where he might want stroll to.

In any case, make a point to reward him differentially as per how close he hits ground zero.

Offer one treat for doing it outside rapidly, two treats for doing it inside, state, five yards of the doggy latrine, three gifts for inside two yards, and five treats for a pinpoint center.

Issues

In case you're utilizing the strategies above, yet having problems with house-soiling or house annihilation following a number of weeks. Go easy and iterate the steps.

Errorless Chew toy Training

Chew toy stuffing

An old chew toy turns out to be interesting and energizing when loaded down with nourishment.

In the case that you use kibble from your young pup's ordinary day by day apportion to make sure your little dog won't put on weight.

To watch your small dog's waistline, heart, and liver, it is essential to limit the utilization of treats in preparing. Use kibble as draws and prizes for encouraging fundamental habits and hold freeze-dried liver treats for beginning housetraining, for meeting kids, men, and outsiders, as an embellishment for stuffing Kongs (see underneath), and as an infrequent significant stake compensation for particularly high conduct.

Kong Stuffing 101

The fundamental guideline of Kong stuffing is to guarantee that some nourishment turns out effectively to a quick prize for your little dog for at first reaching his chew toy.

Bits of food turn out over an extensive period to intermittently compensate your young dog for proceeding to bite, and the absolute best bits never turn out, so your pup never loses intrigue.

Squish a little bit of freeze-dried liver in the small gap in the tip of the Kong so your dog will always be able to get it out.

Smear somewhat nectar around within the Kong, top it off with kibble, and afterward close the massive gap with crossed puppy bread rolls.

There are various innovative minor departure from essential Kong stuffing. One of my preferred plans includes dampening your young dog's kibble, spooning it into the Kong, and afterward placing it in the cooler medium-term—a Kongsicle! Your dog will cherish it.

How about we put everything on hold to consider all the terrible things your dog won't do in the condition that he is discreetly connected with his chew toys.

He won't bite improper family unit and nursery things. He won't be a recreational barker. (He will, in any case, bark when outsiders come to the house. however, he won't go throughout the day just barking.)

And he won't be going here and there, worrying, and stirring himself up whenever left at home alone.

The great thing about showing a young dog to appreciate biting chew toys is that this movement prohibits numerous other options and irritating little dog practices.

A stuffed Kong is extraordinary compared to other pressure relievers, particularly for on edge, passionate, and enthusiastic puppies. (A Kong for a dog is likewise a standout amongst other pressure relievers for the proprietor.)

There is no single gadget that so effectively thus counteracts or settle such a significant number of unfortunate propensities and conduct issues.

Settle Down and Shush

High on the instructive motivation is to show your puppy that there are times for play and times for calm. In particular, you need to show the youngling to settle down and shush for brief periods.

Your life will be progressively serene, and your puppy's life will be less upsetting once he discovers that continuous minimal, calm minutes are the name of the game in his new home.

Be careful the snare of covering your new little dog with relentless consideration and fondness during his early days at home, for then he will cry, bark, and fuss when taken off alone around evening time or during the daytime when you are grinding away, and the kids are at school.

The puppy is desolate! It's the pup's first time alone without his caring mom, littermates, or human friendship.

You can genuinely facilitate your little dog's tension by getting him used to settling down alone during his initial days in the house. Keep in mind that initial introductions are significant and dependable.

Additionally, remember that the average rural young dog will probably spend numerous hours and days left to his very own gadgets.

So it is really advantageous to show the puppy how to invest energy independent from anyone else. Something else, the young dog may become on edge when taken off alone and grow hard-to-break biting, woofing, burrowing, and getting away inclination.

At the point when you are at home, limit your little dog to his doggy cave with bunches of chew toys for housetraining, chew toy preparing, and showing the puppy to settle down calmly and joyfully.

It is essential to let your young dog be alone for brief periods when you are home to show him how to appreciate his very own conversation when disregarded at home.

I am personally not upholding disregarding dogs for significant periods. In any case, it is a reality of cutting edge life that numerous little dog proprietors venture out from home every day to work professionally, so it is entirely reasonable to set up the puppy for this.

At the point when you are at home, the key is momentary imprisonment. The thought isn't to bolt up the little dog for a considerable length of time but instead to instruct him to settle down quickly in an assortment of settings and be limited for a variable time. However, for the most part, it'll be genuinely short periods.

Accordingly, the puppy builds up a solid chew toy propensity directly from the beginning, when there is nothing else really valuable within reach to bite.

Also, let me rehash: A pup cheerfully engrossed with a stuffed chew toy isn't wrecking family unit items and furniture, and isn't yapping.

At the point when you are at home, it is likewise a smart thought to once in a while keep your dog to his little dog den (long haul constrainment region) as a training run for your nonattendance.

Incidental long haul control when you are at home enables you to screen your puppy's conduct so you have some thought how he will act when you are not available.

In the case that your pup barks or cries when bound to his short-or long haul constrained territory, reward-train him to rest unobtrusively.

Sit by your pup's container or directly outside his young dog den and occupy yourself by perusing a book, taking a shot.

Overlook your little dog while he hums, yet each time he quits yapping, promptly acclaim him smoothly and offer a bit of kibble. After about six reiterations, dynamically increase the shush time required for each progressive bit of kibble—two seconds, three seconds, five, eight, fifteen, twenty, and so forth.

From there on, occasionally acclaim and prize your dogs like clockwork or something like that in the case that he remains resting discreetly if yapping is as yet an issue following a long time.

What to Do at Nighttime

You pick where your little dog dozes around evening time. In a case that you need your small dog in his long haul constrainment region on a medium-term, or in a puppy carton in the kitchen, or your room, that is fine.

Or otherwise, in a case that you need the puppy fastened in his bed adjacent to your bed, which is fine as well.

What is significant, however, is that the little dog is bound to a bit of zone and settles down rapidly and discreetly. Offer the little dog a shrewdly stuffed chew toy, and he will probably bite himself to stay in bed no time by any stretch of imagination.

When you have housetrained and chew toy prepared your little dog, and he has figured out how to settle down rapidly and unobtrusively, you may enable your puppy to pick where he might want to rest—inside, outside, upstairs, down the stairs, in your room, or your bed—similarly as long as his decision is approved by you.

It is a smart thought to rehearse the evening schedule during the daytime when you are conscious and in an amiableness.

Try not to stand by to prepare your dog until you are drained and prepared for bed, and your grumpy mind is scarcely working.

During the daytime, work on having your pup settle down in his bed or case in a similar room as you and in various places with the goal that he becomes acclimated to resting alone.

Should your little dog cry in the evening, beware of him at regular intervals. Whisper to him and stir him tenderly for a moment and afterward hit the hay. Yet, don't try too hard.

The thought is to console your pup, not to make him feel sober. Likewise, don't go directly to rest, for you'll most likely be keeping an eye on your dog for the following ten minutes.

When the little dog, in the end, nods off, I think that it's pleasant to monitor him as well as stroke him for about 4-5mins. Many individuals dare not do this for dread; they will wake the little critter, yet it has consistently worked admirably for me.

If you pursue the above daily practice, you'll see it will take under seven evenings before your little dog figures out how to rest rapidly and discreetly.

Sitting, and so on.

I surmise there would be more than a couple of disillusioned proprietors in a case that I didn't, in any event, say something regarding preparing your dog to sit. It seems merely so natural.

Ask your pup, "Can you want to figure out how to sit on request?" and afterward move a bit of kibble all over before his nose. If your dog gestures in understanding, at that point, you're both prepared to continue.

Speak the word "Sit" and afterward move the kibble upwards and in reverse along with the highest point of his gag. Also giving a directional movement showing it to sit.

As the young dog turns upward to pursue the kibble, he will plunk down sitting. Quite straightforward? Yes.

Explicitly, "Little dog, Down" and with another bit of kibble among finger and thumb, bring down your hand, palm descending, to only before the dog's two forepaws.

Your little dog will bring down his nose to examine the kibble and afterward bring down his forequarters with the side of his gag on the floor to snuggle under your hand. Move the kibble somewhat towards your dog's chest, and his backside will thud down.

Explicitly state, "Young pup, Stand," and push the kibble ahead away from your little dog. (You may need to sway the kibble a little to reactivate the puppy.)

Hold the treat at nose level, however, lower it a touch when your puppy stands up and begins to sniff; generally, your puppy will sit when he stands.

You presently have a go at affixing a couple of directions together. Back up two or three stages, state, "Dog, Come Here," and wave the kibble.

Excitedly acclaim your dog as he approaches, and afterward request that he sit and rests before offering the kibble.

Three reactions for one bit of kibble—not terrible, eh? Presently have your dog come, relax, and rests the same number of times as there are extra minutes in the day or the same amount of bits of kibble in the dog's supper.

Drearily practice the over three position changes in arbitrary arrangements—Sit-Down, Sit-Stand, Down-Stand, and so forth.

Perceive what number of position changes your little dog is happy to accomplish for only one nourishment reward and to what extent you can keep the young dog in each area (short stays) before giving every nourishment award.

For some odd reason, the fewer treats you provide, and the more you keep each gift in your grasp, the better your little dog will learn.

CHAPTER EIGHT

FUNDAMENTALS OF TRAINING AND BRAIN GAMES FOR DOGS

The big three necessities of life food, shelter, and clothing are nothing contrasted with the enormous three dog preparation: *Timing, Consistency, and Motivation*. Furnished with these three standards, you can prepare a dog to do pretty much anything.

In a situation that you are continually experiencing issues in preparing, or it appears the puppy is confounded, inquire as to whether you have completed necessary things. There is no hazy area for hounds. Your preparation must be apparent.

Timing; A puppy takes a time of 1.3 seconds wherein to connect a reason with an action. This implies the familiar maxim, "you must catch them in the demonstration," which is true.

A dog accepts he is being amended or applauded for anything that he is doing right now.

Mutts embrace the here and now. The significance of timing has incredible ramifications in preparing. It implies you have to observe firmly enough that you see mix-ups or triumphs precisely when they happen and can either commend or address them in a split second.

Standing by longer than 1.3 seconds may make perplexity in your puppy because of the time slack in correspondence.

Consistency; There is no hazy area for hounds. Your preparation must be precise. A standard is a standard. For instance, if you don't need your puppy to hop upon you, you should reliably strengthen that guideline.

Let's assume I have gotten an advancement at work, and I am feeling extraordinary. I get back home and let **Trip** hop on me since I am so upbeat.

I scratch his head and reveal to him he's an incredible kid. The following day, let's imagine Smitty, my most outstanding opponent from bookkeeping, had stopped in my parking space at noon, and I needed to stroll from the rear of the part.

Going back to my vehicle, I stepped in a grape bubble gum whose smell overwhelmed the inside of my VW Bug while in transit to the house.

At that point, as I stroll in the entryway **_Trip_** hops on me. I am feeling horrendous so I blow up with him for hopping up.

Presently miserable Trip is confounded and doesn't realize whether he's coming or going on the issue of hopping up. Would it be a good idea for him to hop up, or would it be a good idea for him to not?

You should be bright and high contrast in your preparation. You should be 100% predictable. This will bring about a dog that has a sense of security and trusting inside all around characterized rules.

Motivation/Inspiration; in basic terms, consider it along these lines, positivity makes conduct proceed and negativity makes it stop. You impart to your dog while preparing (and every other time too) with commendation and prizes when they are progressing admirably.

Subsequently, the practices you reward will begin to happen all the more frequently. You speak with rectifications (verbal, rope, sound, and so on) when they commit errors or are defying your characterized guidelines.

Thus, the practices you wrong won't happen as frequently. Both commendation (prizes) and amendments must be persuasive to the dog. You need your correspondence to be necessary.

That implies your acclaim or rewards must be sufficient that the puppy is propelled to take a step at it later on.

For instance, if a dog doesn't prefer to be whistled at and your prize for accomplishing something effectively is petting, that isn't prize isn't positive enough for that puppy. Make a point to utilize the reinforcement that your puppy reacts to.

Your adjustments should be sufficient to diminish or quench unwanted conduct. In a perfect world, finding *Trip* doing the right practices is the best method to prepare him.

Practice regularly!

The Four Stages of Learning happens when your dog sets up a connection between the conduct and the results. For instance, when a puppy barks at a strange gate entry (for example, the mailman), the yapping would be reduced as the stimulus (the mailman) evacuates.

You will experience a procedure with each new exercise you show your puppy. It requires some investment to instruct him to perform dependably and accurately. Mutts need three to a half year of reiteration and support to build up conduct in long haul memory.

This implies you should keep on working with your dog after your acquiescence class, exercises, or in-pet house preparing is finished, if you need the preparation to "stick." The longer you take to show activity and fortify it, the better your puppy will perform.

Beneath, we will cover the four periods of learning: *Securing – Showing, Programmed – Fluency, Application – Generalizing, and Continuous - Maintenance.* In the situation that you need a dog that for every situation to be accurate, reliable, it is indispensable that you expend every one of these means.

Securing - Showing During the demonstrating stage, we give the dog the entirety of the important data expected to play out a particular conduct. The coach ought to have a mental image of what the last conduct ought to resemble.

We help the dog settle on the right choices using prompts in an interruption-free condition. Show your puppy what you need him to do.

To achieve this, utilization of your rope, hands, nourishment and different apparatuses to direct your puppy through the practices are all you need.

For instance, in a situation that I am instructing **Trip** to sit, I will give the sit order once, and pursue the direction by tenderly controlling Fido into a sit.

Directly at the moment my dog sits, I will reward him with the goal that he knows precisely what he did to fulfill me. There are no remedies in this stage.

Try not to anticipate that your puppy should understand and effectively perform directions before they have been indicated what it is you need. Use nourishment and commendation liberally during the indicating stage.

Preparing ought to be done in an imprint Training Information Guide directions before they have been indicated what it is you need. Use nourishment and recognition liberally during the indicating stage.

Preparing ought to be done in a region as interruption-free as conceivable as there is no compelling reason to make things increasingly troublesome as of now.

Redundancy and persistence are critical. At the point when your puppy starts to foresee what you need and perform without your assistance, then you realize he is starting to comprehend.

Programmed - Fluency In this stage, we offer the puppy the chance to give us what we have shown him - a calendar timing in for positive actions the right reactions and gentle discipline for negative reactions.

(Mellow neckline direction or No Reward Marker). Continuously remember great planning with input is basic.

When the puppy has a familiarity with specific conduct, then you can improve the speed of a reaction and clean the last picture. At the point when you have 80% or above achievement rate move to the following stage.

During this stage, the puppy ought to comprehend the direction with the goal that he has a reasonable possibility of performing admirably.

On the condition that your dog doesn't comprehend a direction, looks bewildered, terrified, or over and over commits errors, you ought to return to the instructing stage.

Begin to wean the dog of any language you are utilizing, for example, bowing down when you request that your puppy goes "Down."

If you are utilizing nourishment treats to snare your dog, start to utilize the nourishment as a prize for occupation all around done, and not as a guide. Chain direction ought to be directional.

This implies your direction should assist the dog by doing what we are inquiring about. A sit revision is a pull straight up on the neckline with the goal that it controls the dog into a sit. Our down amendment is toward the ground, and so forth.

Application – Summing up to organize is the place you make your puppy's promise to playing out an activity and when your dog discovers that he ought to play out these activities since they are fun as well as because he must do as such. Prize your dog when he accomplishes something right. Give your dog mellow remedies when he commits errors.

It seems as though we are stating, "Indeed, sit implies sit in any event, and when a feline walks passed." The objective is to have a dog that will hold a down during an evening gathering in any event.

During the Generalization, organize open your mutts to every unique circumstance where they will gain from it. Set them up for progress.

By doing this, we have a chance to prepare a dog who will perform under regular interruption not just on

Tuesday evenings at duty classes. It is additionally significant that you don't constantly set your dog up to lose.

Even though they are further developed at this stage, commendation and achievement are as yet essential fixings to Fido's result.

Ensure Fido isn't losing without wins. If he is, that is a decent sign that you are pushing forward excessively quick.

Continuous-Maintenance; taking the show out is a long-lasting procedure.

The dog is cleaned and performs sensibly predictable moves. To keep up a reaction, long haul intermittent remarks for wanted practices must happen.

Mind games for dogs

Presentation

Drilled puppies fall into difficulty. Brilliant and dynamic mutts get into naughtiness. Without enough to keep them involved, dogs of different kinds will go independently employed: striking the receptacle, delving openings in the nursery, yelping for consideration.

This booklet was motivated by one of my mutts— Jackson. At five years old months, he required broad medical procedures for a hip issue.

The post-operation stage implied much-decreased exercise and gave me the test of how to keep a youthful and excited little dog involved—while preventing my shoes safe from being bitten!

Mutts in the wild face astound each day. They need to discover nourishment, water, and a protected spot to rest.

Our puppies have this given: they get their food in a dish, their water is continuously accessible, and their comfortable container sits in the corner. Puppies need to think carefully to keep involved, glad and well-adjusted.

Games:
- **Fun with nourishment**
- **Empty head**
- **Message in a container Just like that!**
- **What's in the case?**
- **Indoor find the stowaway**
- **Biting—what's hot, what's not**
- **Your puppy's on/off switch**
- **Motivation control**
- **Settle down**
- **Stunning labyrinths**
- **Focusing on**
- **Beginning**
- **Messing around while focusing on**
- **Open-air interests**
- **Hustling circuits**
- **Rollover**
- **Puppy masters**
- **The 101 game**
- **Take the IQ test**

- **Fun with nourishment**

As opposed to giving your dog nourishment in a dish, why not make him work for it? You needed to work to get it!

Nourishment in a dish takes just seconds to eat. Food dissipated in your nursery, or even around your home, can take numerous minutes to discover and expand, keeping your puppy occupied pleasantly while guaranteeing that he's utilizing those bits of his mind that would somehow or another go unexercised.

Empty head

Begin by dissipating your puppy's nourishment in a little region—ideally on a smooth surface so he can without much of a stretch, see it and discover it.

When your dog has the hang of this, take a stab at dispersing it in a more extensive region; at that point, proceed onward to tossing it onto the grass—which implies your puppy should chase with his nose, not merely his eyes.

Wet nourishment doesn't generally fit dissipate sustaining. However, you could, without any or stress or stretch, adjust the thought by placing your dog's apportion into a few little holders and concealing them around the house and nursery. Your puppy will adore finding his nourishment and eating it each segment in turn.

In a situation that your puppy is a genuine master at discovering his supper, you can make it to a higher degree a test by dispersing it under hedges or in the long grass. You can even make a 'nourishment trail' by dropping the bits of nourishment in a long, irregular line.

My puppies love this game—in truth, they are entirely frustrated in a situation that I give them their supper in a bowl.

Then again, you can put your dog's wet nourishment inside a Kong or two and enable him to bite and lick the toy to get it out. You can even freeze the Kong with your puppy's supper inside for a reviving riddle on hot days. This is best delighted in outside!

Group control

If there's a condition that you have more than one puppy, be mindful so as not to build rivalry around nourishment by dispersing bolstering them together.

Instead, busy one puppy, while the other is outside looking for his food. On the other hand, feed them in isolated rooms.

Message in a container

Another mental soundness saver for when you need to jump on, yet your puppy needs something to do.

Pick a reasonable size and kind of void plastic water bottle. Ensure the sort folds—and doesn't part—when you crush it.

Put a portion of your dog's dry nourishment into the container and shake it to get his attention.

For the initial few attempts, include some super titbits as well, for example, little solid shapes of cheddar or free meat so that he can smell that lovely things are inside.

What's in the case?

Urging your puppy to think carefully has various advantages.

The first is that in a case that you are locked in with him in explaining astounds which you have made, and he will be far more reluctant to go searching for riddles to understand without anyone else, for example, how to purge the kitchen receptacle or get away from the nursery.

The second is that critical thinking requires mental exertion, and even though this is not a substitute for giving your dog physical exercise, it can channel vitality that some way or another should be singed off somewhere else.

I gauge that drawing in your puppy in agreeable personality games for twenty minutes can be proportionate to an hour of physical exercise—and your dog will be joyfully worn out toward its finish.

This isn't valuable for youthful mutts with vast vitality, yet leaving out hounds whose activity is limited, because they have a medical issue.

It's additionally extraordinary for establishing the frameworks of the quiet center that puppies with conduct issues frequently need.

Stimulate that mind

Start this riddle by setting the cup or mug topsy turvy on a harsh surface, for example, a covered part or on a floor covering.

When your dog is sure with how to unravel the puzzle of the shrouded nourishment, make it progressively troublesome by putting the cup on a hard or elusive surface.

The container will, at that point, slide, taking the treat with it, and your dog should make sense of another arrangement.

1. Turn an old cup or mug topsy turvy and let your dog watch you place some incredibly delectable treats underneath. These should be enticing, for example, small bits of cheddar or cooked chicken.

2. Try not to enable your puppy to turn out how to get the treats. This is intended to challenge his cerebrum all things considered! If you genuinely need to mediate because your puppy is losing interest, at that point, prop the edge of the cup on one of the treats so he can smell and taste it. On the other hand, change the treatment to a higher evaluation one.

3. Time to what extent it takes your dog to turn out how to get the treats from under the cup. A few puppies utilize their noses, others their paws—and one incredibly astute Dobermann young dog mostly

got the cup by the handle with his teeth, deliberately set it down, and afterward ate the treats. Virtuoso!

What's in the crate?

Boxes are a modest and fun approach to make indoor burrowing riddles and games for your puppy. Continuously watch that whatever crates you use are liberated from tape or staples that may make hurt your dog.

Indoor burrowing

Many mutts need to burrow. It's not merely that they like to—they need to.

A few breeds, for example, Dachshunds, for instance, were reared to burrow when chasing for prey, and this implies the drive is 'hard-wired' in their cerebrums. Different breeds may experience a burrowing 'stage,' especially.

If your puppy is a little interested placing his front paws into the case, toss a few treats in with the goal that he needs to lean in to get them.

Fight the temptation to get him and lift him in—this may put him off significantly more and squanders a decent chance to let him work something out for himself.

These dogs may necessarily be having a fabulous time transforming your grass into a tip and need a fitting outlet for their conduct briefly.

Now put a couple of more treats into the case. However, this time spread them up with an old towel; some scrunched up paper or a bit of cardboard about a similar size as the floor of the crate. Urge your dog to burrow for his prize.

Indoor find the stowaway

Dogs love to scan for things, particularly those that are inquisitive, for example, nourishment and toys.

"Indoor find the stowaway" can be an incredible method for showing your puppy to utilize his nose just as his eyes to chase for things—and can be a helpful method to practice his mind when it's coming up.

Strikingly, the real demonstration of your dog pausing while you conceal the toy or nourishment additionally causes him to learn poise and can improve his "pause" or "remain" practices as well.

Many mutts have a most loved toy that you can stow away for them to discover, yet in a situation that you are only beginning with a little dog or a rehomed hound, it very well may be simpler to start with nourishment covered up inside a holder.

Nuts and bolts

Overlap down the finish of a can move cylinder and pop several flavorful, rotten treats inside. Overlay down the top. Let your puppy sniff the bottle with the goal that he knows there's something inside.

If you've made your puppy pause or remain, request that he do as such while you shroud the cylinder someplace in the same room. He should not move— that is cheating.

When you have concealed the cylinder, stroll back to your puppy before giving him a discharge order that guides him to discover it.

A few mutts may require consolation, yet attempt to let him find out it all alone. When your dog finds the cylinder, urge him to get it so you can open it and give him the treats.

Recover versus devastate

If there's a condition that your puppy is a loo-move destroyer, have a go at placing the treats in to speed up textured pencil case. He'll have to carry it to you for help with the zip!

Proceeding onward

When your puppy has the hang of searching for things in dull concealing spots, biting what's not.

Chewing a toy with nourishment stuffed inside is a decent and sensible personality game for hounds.

Be that as it may, not all bite toys are made equal. Many that we may think would be compelling are dull as dishwater to hounds.

While different things that we wouldn't consider to be deserving of a subsequent look are a puppy's concept of paradise. Anyway, in your puppy's eyes it's what's hot.

Different top choices

Other great biting things include Nylabones: produced using nylon, they are enhanced to make them progressively tantalizing and are sheltered in any event, for solid chewers, however, supplant them consistently to guarantee that little pieces don't get a bit off.

Best evaded

Albeit a few owners depend on rawhide bites, they can be tricky. They can get stuck in the rear of the dog's throat, obstructing the air route.

Cooked bones ought to never be encouraged to hounds as there is a danger of them fragmenting— which may cause damage to the gut.

CHAPTER NINE

KNOWLEDGE ON REINFORCEMENT FOR DOGS

Even though habituation continues most effectively with improvements that are mellow, gentle boosts are once in a while an issue in hound preparing the upgrades that upset the dogs' exhibition.

Which is by actuating trepidation and uneasiness are regularly exceptionally serious.

For example, shots or running plane motors. Be that as it may, habituation to even significant or startling upgrades can be accomplished utilizing a chain of command of power — a scale on which upgrade force increments steadily from low to high. A down to earth approach to diminish the force of clamor improvements is by presenting the dog to them from a considerable span.

For instance, the puppy is first given the sound of a running plane motor a good distance of 500 meters, where it shows just mellow tension. When this nervousness vanishes through habituation, at that point, the dog is moved to the following level in the chain of command by strolling to inside maybe 400 meters of the fly motor.

When any tension reactions have habituated, at that point, the handler draws the dog nearer, etc. By acquainting the dog with startling improvements at a degree of force that is low to such an extent that it incites next to zero dread reaction, and by moving step by step from one phase on the pecking order of force to the following, the mentor prepares the puppy to display little dread in the nearness of even exceptionally extraordinary situations.

Counter conditioning. Habituation can be quickened by blending a substantial, lovely increase with the dread initiating improvement.

To again utilize the past model, if the hound is scared of a running plane motor, its dread can be balanced by introducing the puppy with a substantial, lovely upgrade like nourishment or a ball.

This method is called counterconditioning, and ought to be joined with the utilization of orders of force.

This is because if the dog fears the moving motor, it will disregard the nourishment or a ball when it is near the engine — it will be too reluctant even to consider eating or play.

In this way, counterconditioning is led at separations dynamically ever nearer to the motor, starting a right way off incredible enough with the goal that the puppy's uneasiness is effectively balanced by its pleasure at being given nourishment or a ball. At each phase of the chain of command.

(for example good ways from the fly motor), it is fundamental that the mentor utilizes the dog's conduct as the proportion of when to continue to the following stage so that counterconditioning continues at a pace fit for the individual dog.

Moving too rapidly "up" the chain of importance (for example closer to the stream motor) won't create a decrease in dread, and could even counter condition the nourishment or ball, decreasing the dog's pleasurable reaction to these.

(Note: Counterconditioning is really a type of traditional molding — to be clarified underneath — yet it is presented here for congruity in the discourse of techniques of dread decrease.)

Unconstrained recuperation. Dread reactions are entirely robust and tenacious and can reappear significantly after broad habituation "treatment."

This is because habituation incorporates specific momentary procedures that "wear off" following a couple of moments or hours, and it is typical for a habituated reaction to re-appear somewhat between instructional courses.

In this way, a dog may show no dread of an upgrade before one day's over's instructional meeting. However, show recuperated dread toward the start of the following session. This wonder is called unconstrained recuperation.

For instance, a puppy habituated to an uproarious clamor like an air blower (for example shows no dread), may show some trepidation whenever it experiences the blower.

It is imperative to comprehend that in any event, when habituation and counterconditioning are accurately applied, the dread reaction will frequently reappear.

Be that as it may, from session to session, there ought to be less and less unconstrained recuperation of the dread reaction.

Disadvantageous Habituation

Habituation may diminish as opposed to building the dog's viability because compelling presentation in a working puppy relies on a certain degree of enthusiasm for, and responsiveness to, natural improvements.

A puppy that is generally new to identification tasks may convey severe and centered hunt conduct since it is invigorated and energized by the unique learning circumstance.

Yet after more experience, the dog may get languid and seem "exhausted."

The best defense against such an undesirable behavior of the dog's delight in its work is to infuse however much assortment as could reasonably be expected into the dog's everyday schedule.

For example, an identifier dog ought to be prepared in whatever number various areas as would be prudent, and an assortment of multiple prize items and games ought to be utilized as reinforces.

Furthermore, unconstrained recuperation can be used for help to prepare — if the puppy isn't worked for a timeframe, there ought to be some recuperation in its delight in work.

Traditional molding

Traditional molding is the learning of enthusiastic and reflexive reactions through the development of mental relationships between upgrades.

In any case, after the puppy is controlled by specialists and infused with a needle, it might relate the look, smell, and sound of the vet facility with physical restriction and the torment of the infusion, with the goal that whenever it is taken in for a method the center upgrades are never again unbiased — they will evoke a similar dread that physical limitation and infusion do.

In old-style molding (additionally called Pavlovian casting), the dog learns a connection between two occasions or upgrades.

One of these boosts is an "unbiased" or insignificant boost that a dog would regularly give little consideration to. This improvement is known as the molded boost, or CS since it can create substantial conduct just because of molding.

The different development is a naturally significant boost that a dog gives a great deal of consideration typically to — like nourishment.

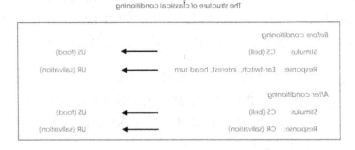

In the traditional model, the Russian researcher Ivan Pavlov instructed puppies to salivate in reaction to the ringing of a ringer.

Pavlov did this by over and again matching a chime (CS) and some nourishment (US), displaying them near one another in time.

A credulous dog regularly reacts to the ringing of a little ringer by only jerking its ears or looking towards the commotion.

Be that as it may, a bit of nourishment can make the puppy show a lot of substantial conduct like fervor, salivation, burrowing, pawing, biting, and eating.

This extraordinary conduct brought about by introduction to the US is known as the unconditioned reaction or UR. Through old-style molding, the CS and the US become related in the dog's "mind," so conduct that is usually activated by the US (the UR) becomes activated somewhat by the CS too.

At the point when a CS builds up the capacity to trigger conduct that is ordinarily brought about by the US, this scholarly reaction is known as the adapted reaction or CR.

In this manner, in the long run, Pavlov's puppy discovered that the chime anticipated nourishment and started to salivate in light of the chime (CR).

Applying traditional molding

The best technique for the old-style frame includes displaying the unbiased boost/order (CS) preceding the naturally significant improvement (US).

In this way, if the handler wishes to prepare the dog to feel surprised and restless in light of "no!" at that point, a successful technique is hold up until the dog takes part in some mischief like sniffing the rubbish. The handler at that point gives the "No!" sign, and tosses a chain gag neckline against the waste can help with the goal that it makes a dull sound about a second after the "No!".

Initially, "No!" (CS) implies little to the puppy and delivers small changes in conduct. The unsavory clamor (US) is compelling and causes a solid frighten or freezing reaction (UR).

Matching the "No!" with the undesirable noise shows the dog to surprise/freeze because of "No!" (CR) inside one or a very hardly any CS-US pairings. Afterward, when the puppy is occupied with trouble-making, the handler can utilize the "No!" order, making the dog surprise/freeze (which serves to hinder the unwanted action), and the controller would then be able to review the puppy.

The puppy will before long figure out how to avoid practices and items when it hears the "No!" order (old-style molding) and comes back to its handler for acclaiming.

At the point when the CS and the US have turned around, with the goal that the US goes before the CS, this is known as an in reverse molding methodology.

Next to zero learning happens during reverse molding. Subsequently, even numerous redundancies of a preparation preliminary wherein the dog are frightened with a loud commotion and afterward hears a "No!" may not deliver a frighten reaction when "No!" is given independently from anyone else.

Eradication of traditionally adapted reactions. Not everything a puppy learns through traditional molding is attractive. For example, on the off chance that a brutal redress is given the first run through a chain gag neckline is set on the puppy,

The creature will most likely show hindrance and nervousness whenever a chain neckline is set on its neck. Bothersome traditionally adapted reactions can be debilitated or, on the other hand, even nullified by exhibiting the CS more than once without blending it with the US, making the CR step by step decline in quality.

CONSEQUENCES

There are two fundamental classes of outcomes in instrumental molding

Methodology—support and discipline.

Reinforcement is a consequence that empowers or reinforces earlier conduct.

Instances of reinforces are nourishment, access to a toy, or a gesture of congratulations. Any of these, at the point when given to the dog after it sits, will in general, reinforce his actions.

Nourishment, toys, pats on the head are strengthening feats since they are charming to the pup.

These sorts of outcomes are classified as "positive reinforces" In any case, unsavory occasions can likewise go about as reinforces.

For instance, the handler can strengthen conduct by methods for an undesirable opportunity like a jolt on the rope, by retaining the snap when the dog sits.

In this model, there is an adverse reaction rule between sitting conduct and a surprise on the neckline — if the puppy sits, there will be no twitch.

Even though the jolt itself is horrendous, the nonappearance of the snap is a "fantastic situation" and will, under legitimate conditions, serve to strengthen sitting conduct.

This sort of reinforce is known as a "negative reinforce." Discipline is a result that demoralizes or debilitates earlier behavior.

Models of punishers are snaps on the (neckline remedies) or knock on the nose. Both of these, when controlled to a dog after it makes trouble, for instance, breaking the down-stay position without consent, will in general, debilitate down-stay-breaking conduct. Neckline rectifications and knocks on the nose are rebuffing because they are horrendous. These sorts of outcomes are called incomprehensibly, "positive punishers." Nonetheless, charming occasions can likewise go about as punishers.

The handler can rebuff unfortunate conduct by retaining or removing an attractive boost like recognition and petting.

For instance, if the puppy will come in general, hop up on the handler when it is energized, hopping up can be rebuffed by retaining applause and consideration.

In this model, there is an adverse reaction rule between hopping up conduct and acclaim what's more, petting — if the puppy hops up, it won't get recognition or petting. Since the approval and petting are charming, their nonattendance is a "sub-par situation" and will under the best possible conditions, rebuff hopping up conduct. This is called "negative discipline."

Utilization of the expressions "positive" and "negative."

The terms positive and negative characterize the four potential outcomes of instrumental conduct — positive reinforcement, negative support, positive discipline, and negative control.

Be that as it may, "positive" and "negative" utilized in this sense have nothing to do with whether the method is charming or upsetting for the dog. A regularly abused articulation is "negative support," because non-clinicians decipher "negative" as significantly bad awful or upsetting.

In this way, negative support is usually utilized just as it was synonymous with physical discipline, yet it is not. The terms positive and negative in this setting allude to the idea of the reaction rule (additionally alluded to as a possibility) between the dog's reaction and the result.

Essential and Auxiliary Reinforcement and Discipline.

Numerous prizes and disciplines are naturally incredible boosts, for example, the chance to eat or a problematic snap on the neckline. In the language of traditional molding, they are called unconditioned upgrades (USA).

In the language of instrumental embellishment, they are called essential reinforcers or essential punishers.

Mutts react promptly and positively to these upgrades without being instructed to do so. Be that as it may, a few prizes and disciplines initially have little impact on a puppy's conduct.

Called optional reinforcers and punishers, they don't get powerful until they have been related to essential reinforcers or punishers.

Auxiliary reinforcers gain their capacity to fortify and energize conduct by being related (through old-style molding forms) with essential reinforcers.

For example, little dogs likely don't instinctually appreciate being addressed. They learn to like being treated in an upbeat voice since this voice is related to physical petting and with the introduction of nourishment.

After enough of this molding, words like "Great!" spoken in a glad voice becomes charming improvements. In this manner, the term "Great!" can fortify earlier conduct (if the handler says "Great!" following the dog execution of the task).

Auxiliary punishers gain their capacity to debilitate and demoralize conduct by being related to essential punishers.

For example, "No!" (Spoken in a nonpartisan tone) makes no difference to an undeveloped dog. The word becomes disagreeable because it is related (through old-style molding) with upsetting essential rebuffing occasions like a yank on the neckline.

After enough of this molding, the order "No!" depicts something undesirable. Along these lines, "No!" can rebuff earlier conduct (if the handler says "No!" following the dog executes the behavior).

Utilization of negative reinforcement

Negative reinforcement includes remunerating conduct by retaining impulse.

The exemplary model in working puppy preparing is the "out" in which the dog discharges a fomenter or a prize item (for example, an elastic ball) on order.

Albeit a handler employments of any accessible, uplifting feedback to compensate the puppy for discharging neatly (for example acclaim, prompt re-chomp, and so on.), the "out" is regularly taught and kept up mainly through the organization of negative reinforcement. In this way, if the puppy discharges neatly on direction, it isn't amended with a yank on the gag neckline.

Every one of the four of the standards expressed above concerning physical discipline additionally applies to negative reinforcement. Also, the accompanying terms and definitions ought to be comprehended.

Break preparing. Getaway is an underlying phase of negative reinforcement preparing during which the puppy figures out how to end or stop a condition of uneasiness by executing some actual conduct.

For instance, during the break phase of preparing, the direction "Out!" is good for nothing. The puppy doesn't yet comprehend that "Out!" implies a neckline remedy will happen in the case that it doesn't discharge.

Consequently, on the principal preliminary, when the handler gives the "Out!" order, the puppy will most likely keep gnawing.

The controller, at that point, applies a neckline adjustment until the puppy discharges the nibble, applauding the dog once it has released. The following preliminary or two will continue similarly. However, the puppy is learning.

During this stage, the puppy figures out how to expect the adjustment when it hears the order "Out!" and it additionally figures out how to "turn off" or end the change by discharging the chomp.

This departure learning is significant. A puppy that doesn't know precisely how it can "turn off" impulse will be confounded and worried by amendments, and may take part in unseemly practices to attempt to end uneasiness, for example, dodging or on the other hand gnawing the handler.

If an unpredictable reaction like strolling at the heel or reviewing to heel is prepared to utilize negative support, there must fundamentally be a phase during which the handler educates the dog to end neckline amendments by setting itself at the heel.

In the case that the creature doesn't know which conduct reaction will end impulse, at that point, neckline remedies will make it move increasingly more unequivocally away from the handler.

It is in this manner fundamental to utilize reward-based figuring out how to persistently encourage the puppy's abilities before applying departure and negative reinforcement systems — to ensure that the dog knows how to play out the ideal practices in the direction.

The dog will, at that point, be prepared to learn rapidly how to end impulse by executing a told conduct with insignificant pressure or disarray. Speedy learning under inspiration will limit the sum and power of physical power required for preparing, and help to render work a joy for both handler and dog.

Evasion is the following phase of negative support preparing during which the dog discovers that notwithstanding ending impulse by executing the actual conduct, it can dodge impulse.

In the case of the out, if the puppy discharges the chomp rapidly on direction, the neckline remedy will never happen.

Once avoidance is thoroughly and cleanly trained, it is validated by the absence of punishment any time the dog activates it on order.

The ultimate objective of effective reinforcement instruction is to achieve any time, with no need for coercion, a correct answer to the order.

That aim has the additional element of working dog discipline that the trainer wants to eliminate the coercion means eventually entirely (e.g., choke collar as well as a leash).

As an example, if a properly trained dog isn't putting on a choke collar or harness, and if the owner is 3 or 4 yards away, a puck should be released cleanly on order.

Furthermore, the trainer will not abandon the coercion means until a successful aversion standard has been met by the puppy, such as a strong reaction to order over a minimum of 4-5 training sessions.

The trainer would be able to advise the dog immediately throughout these error-free training hours, with every equipment needed in order.

When the solution is not reliably given with no use of coercion, the dog will continue to exercise with the trainer who can impose compliance before criteria evasion is achieved and used thoroughly.

Abuse of coaching to flee. A dog's frequent and continuous physical discipline to compel him to conduct tasks is a clear sign that there is no practical thinking.

When the grip collar is being used ten times in succession, for instance, to compel the puppy to release the pressure whenever the "Out Request" is issued, so no progress is made, as well as the dog would never learn to OUT in such method.

Throughout any specified task, the escape step of training must be extremely brief— from one to at most four iterations of the practice performed with adjustments.

With the dog to know how and when to "turn off" the command, this is sufficient. Then it must be transferred efficiently and effectively to aversion continuation where it is issued on request (instead of when the clarification is applied) to prevent correction.

Apart from the incentive of not being punished, the teacher will give the dog fun treats to strive with. For example, the dog is congratulated after a quick, fast out of the ball and encouraged to re-bite as well as juggle with the ball.

THE CONNECTION BETWEEN TRADITIONAL CONDITIONING AND EXPERIMENTAL CONDITIONING

Hardly any preparation for working dogs requires the intentional development of classically trained relationships like in the "No!" order above.

Much of the "actions" during dog sessions are linked to using corrections and brawlers to generate functional conditioning. Contemporary conditioning techniques, though, are essential as much of the dog's training interactions are behind them.

There are numerous ways in which classically trained interactions lead to teaching. For instance, if a trainer offers a training cue to a detector dog (For example, "Ready to work?").

The dog may equate this signal with the ability to hunt for the desired odor and the anticipation of getting a ball before bringing the animal into a target area then issuing the search order.

Your dog will soon start displaying enthusiasm and energetic reactions to the planning signal, encouraging positive quest actions.

The training cue is the CS throughout this instance of operant conditioning. The experience of playing with such a ball is the US, as well as the CR, is the stimulation responses.

POSITIVE REINFORCEMENT

At the point when evasion is totally and neatly instructed, each time the puppy discharges on the direction, it is compensated by the nonattendance of the adjustment.

Rule shirking.

The ultimate objective of negative reinforcement preparing is to verify the right reaction to the direction unfailingly, without the requirement for impulse.

In working puppy training, this objective has the other measurement that the handler plans to in the long run dispose of the methods for motivation (for example, gag neckline and rope).

For instance, a thoroughly prepared puppy should discharge a ball neatly on the direction when it is not wearing a stifle neckline or rope, and when the handler is 3 or 4 meters away. The handler will, in this way not dispose of the methods for impulse until the dog has accomplished a decent evasion model, for example, steady reaction to direction over at any rate four or on the other hand five instructional meetings.

During these blunder free instructional meetings, the handler will be prepared to address the dog in a flash, with all underlying hardware set up.

If there's a condition that the reaction isn't reliably offered without the requirement for impulse, at that point, the dog must proceed to rehearse with the handler remaining by prepared to uphold compliance until rule evasion is acquired and widely repeated.

Rehashed and delayed substantial revision of a puppy to constrain it to complete activities is a personal sign that positive learning isn't occurring.

For instance, if the gag neckline is utilized multiple times straight to restrain the dog from discharging the nibble when the "Out!" direction is given, at that point, there is no advancement and the dog will never figure out how to out along these lines.

The break period of learning in some random exercise ought to be very short — among one and probably four redundancies of the activity with adjustments applied. This is remarkably enough for the puppy to figure out how to "turn off" the correction.

At that point, it ought to be moved quickly and proficiently into evasion preparing, where it discharges on the direction (as opposed to when the revision is applied) to stay away from the change.

Even though conduct learned through negative support preparing can be truly solid and dependable, negative support ought to be trailed by encouraging feedback at whatever point conceivable.

The mentor can give the puppy fantastic awards to work for, notwithstanding the prize of not being revised. For example, after a clean, quick out from the ball, the hound is applauded and permitted to re-chomp the ball and play with it.

The connection between the old-style molding and instrumental molding Next to no working dog preparing includes the conscious production of classically conditioned relationship, as in the case of the "No!" order above.

The vast majority of the "activity" in hound preparing has to do with the utilization of reinforcers and punishers to deliver instrumental molding.

In any case, old-style molding forms are applicable since they are out of sight of most preparing encounters for the puppy.

Traditionally adapted affiliations add to preparing in incalculable manners. For model, if a handler gives an identification hound a planning sign (for example "Prepared to work? Prepared to work?")

Preceding bringing the creature into a hunting territory and giving the pursuit order, the puppy will connect this signal with the chance to scan for target smell and the energy of getting a ball.

The dog will before long start to display enthusiasm and excitement reactions to the readiness signal, empowering energetic search conduct.

In this case of old-style molding, the readiness signal is the CS, the chance to play with a ball in the US, and excitement reactions are the CR.

At the point when your pet is learning another conduct, she ought to be rewarded each time she does the behavior, which implies steadfast support.

It might be essential to utilize a procedure called "molding" with your pet, which involves strengthening something near the typical reaction and at that point, step by step requiring more from your dog before she gets the treat.

For instance, in case you're showing your dog to "shake hands" you may at first prize her for taking her paw off the ground, at that point for lifting it higher, at that point for contacting your hand, at that point for letting you hold her leg, lastly, for really "shaking hands" with you.

Discontinuous fortification can be utilized once your pet has dependably taken in the conduct. From the outset, reward her with the treat three out of each multiple times she does the behavior.

At that point, after some time, reward her about a fraction of the time, at that point about a fraction of the time, etc.

Until you're just fulfilling her infrequently with the treat. Keep on lauding her each time—albeit once your dog has taken in the conduct, your recognition can be less unreserved, for example, a calm, yet positive, "Great puppy."

Use a variable timetable of fortification so that she doesn't get on that. She needs to react to each other time. Your pet will, before long, discover that if she continues acting, in the end, she'll get what she needs—your commendation and an occasional treat.

By getting fortification, you'll see that you're most certainly not perpetually bound to convey a pocketful of treats.

Your dog will before long be working for your verbal applause, since she genuinely wants to satisfy you and realizes that, once in a while, she'll get a treat, as well.

There are numerous little chances to strengthen her conduct. You can make her "sit" then letting her out the entryway afterward (which averts entryway dashing), previously petting her (which forestalls bouncing upon individuals), or then again before sustaining her. Give her a pat or let her lay discreetly by your feet, or slip a treat into a toy when she's biting it rather than your shoe.

PROS AND CONS OF DISCIPLINE

Discipline can be verbal, postural, or physical, and it implies giving your pet something unsavory following she accomplishes something you don't need her to do. The discipline makes it more outlandish that the conduct will happen once more.

To be successful, training must be conveyed while your pet is occupied with the ill manner—as it were, "caught in the process." If the discipline is conveyed as well late, even seconds after the fact, your pet won't relate the subject with the undesired conduct.

Harsh discipline conveyed by you may dissolve your dog's trust. That is the reason training is best when it doesn't come straightforwardly from you. For instance, after your dog makes demonstrations in a bothersome manner, utilize a shake can, an air horn, or keys— in any case, don't cause to notice the way that the commotion comes from you.

In the case that your dog sees her "condition" of you, to convey the discipline, she'll be more probable to maintain a strategic distance from the conduct in any event, when you're nowhere to be found.

Moreover, in case you're past the point of no return in directing it, discipline will appear to be erratic to your dog. She's probably going to turn into dreadful, doubtful, or forceful, which will prompt more conduct issues.

What we people frequently decipher as "liable" looks are agreeable stances by our pets. Creatures don't have an ethical feeling of good and evil, be that as it may, they are skilled at partner your quality, and the nearness of a wreck, with discipline.

If you've attempted discipline and it hasn't worked, you ought to quit utilizing regimen and utilize just encouraging feedback.

What's more, never use physical training that includes some level of uneasiness or torment, which may make your pet chomp to safeguard herself.

Holding skin on the neck as well as shaking your dog or then again performing "alpha moves" (constraining your dog onto her back, what's more, nailing her to the floor) are both prone to result in chomps.

Also, discipline may be related to other upgrades, including individuals that are available at the time the training happens. For instance, a pet who is rebuffed for getting excessively near a little kid may get frightful of, or then again forceful toward, that kid—or toward other kids.

That is the reason physical discipline isn't awful for your pet, and it's likewise terrible for you and others.

CHAPTER TEN

REVOLUTIONARY HOME TRAINING FOR DOGS

This implies your dog can stay inside your home for a reasonable time (around eight hours) without wiping out in it.

Your dog essentially "holds it" until you let him outside to do his business. In a situation that your dog is physically sound and physically developed (which means he is in any event eight months to a year of age) yet he has more than one defecation in the house each couple of months. At that point, he isn't housetrained.

To what extent will it take for me to housetrain my young dog? To show your dog where to dispose of takes just two or three weeks.

Be that as it may, for a youthful dog or pup to be dependable, it necessitates that the dog is adult enough physically to hold off wiping out until a suitable time, or until he can engine himself to the "toilet."

A dog can't be called dependable or housetrained until he is eight months to a year of age and has not had any defecation in the house for at any rate within a month and a half running.

To what degree will my matured-up dog take me to Home-Train?

For a more established dog with terrible potty propensities, or one who has never been housebroken, you can hope to spend around six weeks to about two months (following a severe housebreaking plan), before another standard of conduct is set up.

In a case that you have a more seasoned dog who is beginning to commit errors in the house when he was excellent for quite a long time previously.

Possibly he has a physical issue that keeps him from holding it (if it's not too much trouble have the dog administered at your veterinarian's first before going on a severe housebreaking project) or he didn't ultimately get that he is never to take out in the house.

What Is Paper Preparing? It is one of the most straightforward approach to prepare him.

That implies the new Sunday paper you left down on the floor is a reasonable game, what's more, the coat you haven't hung up yet is the likewise an intelligent game.

The possibility of housetraining is once more, to educate your hound NEVER to wipe out in the house.

Paper preparing isn't the most effortless approach to prepare him. Papermaking a dog in the house and afterward attempting to instruct him to go outside confounds him and takes him any longer to accomplish dependability.

In a case that you live in a condominium or townhouse, you most likely have a little patio or overhang.

Show your dog to kill in a considerable container (like an oil dribble dish utilized in carports; some pet stores convey an enormous dog potty dish only for this reason) has feline litter in it, which is set outside.

That way, you have furnished him with a spot to potty that is outside your home yet is still simple to tidy up.

Alright, since paper preparing is out, shouldn't something be said about instructing him to utilize a dog entryway?

Permitting your little dog or un-housetrained hound, the utilization of a dog entryway does nothing aside from undermining your housetraining for a few reasons.

Number one, you never honestly know whether the dog did his business or not since you were not there to see it. Number two, your dog won't wipe out in the objective territory on his claim since you were not there to give him where it is.

Dog entryways are beautiful to use after your dog is Independent. It will be ideal if you note that in the situation that you are having any animosity or ruinous conduct, a dog entryway isn't prescribed as it gives your dog as well much opportunity.

How Would I tidy up a defecation?

To do this, you will utilize the stand and blotch strategy. Deciphered, this implies either use a wad of paper towels or papers put over the spot and remain on them for around 30 seconds. At that point, discard the papers and apply your compound cleaner.

Let the protein cleaner absorb for about five minutes or whatever the mark suggests. At that point, utilize the stand and smear technique to absorb the abundance dampness.

I have heard that you can instruct your dog to go when you let him know. **How Would I Educate Him?**

This is considered showing your dog an end direction. First, pick a single word or short expression that you will consistently utilize when you need him to go.

Significant decisions are "BETTER GO" "RUSH" "DO YOUR BUSINESS" "DO YOUR THING". Pick something you will be happy with saying in broad daylight since you will need to have your dog actualize on direction!

When you have picked a term, each time you take your dog out to do his business (as he is dispensing with), state his direction, for example, "DO YOUR THING" and commend him for doing as such.

State the order a few times AS HE IS GOING. Make sure to give him a treat when he is done. It will take him around six weeks to about two months of steady work from you before he will begin to perceive the order and wipe out when you state it.

Would i be able to show my dog to utilize just a single zone of the yard? Indeed! This is called preparing your dog to utilize an objective region.

A specific zone is a little segment of your yard in which you need your dog to peruse consistently. Around a six-foot by six-foot region is bounty large enough for a dog.

An objective territory saves money on your finishing, and you don't need to play out the "look for" strategy when you clean the yard. Likewise, your children will acknowledge not having land mines everywhere!

In the first place, pick an order word or short expression that you will consistently utilize when you take him around here.

Target territory directions are "outside" "Latrine" "yard" or whatever else you wish. Next, state the word as you are strolling your dog out to his objective territory.

Ensure you continually utilize the similar name as you help your dog engine to the target territory. Recognizing him as he is motoring out there.

After around six to about two months of preparing this word, you can begin to utilize it to guide your dog to his objective region.

Should he commit an error in the house or another piece of the yard, give him his proper zone order. Make sure to consistently applaud your dog for utilizing the right region in your yard.

Update: When utilizing objective territories, if it's not too much trouble, ensure you keep the zone clean. A few mutts will decline to use an actual area in a situation that it is messy.

To what extent can a Dog "HOLD IT"?

It relies on how old they are! For youthful mutts, a great, dependable guideline to recall is that your dog is ready to hold disposal for the same number of hours as he is on a long stretch of age.

In a case that your dog is two-months-old, he can keep it for as long as two hours at most during the day in a situation that he isn't dynamic.

In the situation your little dog is energetic, he will need to go out more frequently. Around evening time, most dogs can go longer. Most little dogs when they are twelve weeks of age can rest the whole night through without going out.

For full-developed mutts with no physical or partition uneasiness issues, they ought to have the option to go an eight-hour day without a problem, when you have put them on a regular timetable. Recollect that a full-grown hound is in any event eight months to a year old.

I can't shape, or form watch my young pup throughout the day! I need to get things done and work.

In a situation, you have a youthful dog who isn't mature enough to hold it during your workday, or maybe he is as well young to stay asleep from sundown to sunset, at that point, you have to give a sheltered territory sufficiently large so he can take out in one corner and rest in another of the same zone.

Models would be a segment closed off with his box set in one corner, or an activity pen put in a tiled room.

To help with tidying up when you return, you may fix the territory with paper before you leave. In any case, as before long as you get back home, all the paper gets taken up, and you attempt to get your little dog out before any bad occurs.

A superior method to manage leaving a youthful dog for significant periods is to ask a neighbor, a companion, or contract somebody to come once, twice, or even multiple times during the day to allow your little dog to out.

To ask a dog to remain in a tiny territory for a significant period, without the chance to take out, is all things considered getting down to business against your housetraining.

Your young dog will be compelled to wipe out and afterward lay in it. He will, at that point, create unclean propensities and not think about keeping himself and your home clean.

In a situation that you own a young dog that is dispensing within his carton, ensure he is first empty when you put him in it, furthermore, take him out more regularly.

For hounds that need to pass stuff in the carton, you should take away all sheet material also.

Is There Anything Unique I Have To Get Before i Start House Preparing My Dog?

Indeed. You have to arm yourself with the best possible materials, so you are prepared to manage all the conceivable circumstances that may occur.

The pup defecation will occur. However, your principal objective is to anticipate them as much as credible. Get the accompanying things:

1. Chemical cleaner is utilized for tidying up. Ensure you get one explicitly intended for pee/defecation smells and stains.

Try not to utilize vinegar, club pop, or smelling salts to tidy up droppings. This solitary move your dog back to his botch. You will need to ensure you tidy up after each defecation and utilize the protein cleaner in the direct extent to how huge the defecation was.

In the case that Fido peed around a cup's measurement on the rug, you have to pour in any such event one cup on that spot after you have absorbed as a lot of pee as you can.

2. Paper Towels or Papers will be utilized to smudge up the chaos after the cleaner has done its work.

3. Restriction can be alleviated wherever where you wouldn't care less if your dog commits an act as such. It is ideally somewhere that is sheltered (which means he can't stumble into difficulty by biting up things like the rug or, on the other hand, electrical wires), is inside your home, and is sufficiently little, so he attempts to hold disposing of until you let him out.

Mutts have an innate intuition not to soil close to them or where they rest. That is the reason box preparing is as fruitful as a housetraining help.

A few instances of restriction are: a container simply huge enough for him to rests and pivot in, a closed-off segment of the kitchen or another room sufficiently large to pivot and set down, or a little washroom.

So How Would I Start?

Put your dog on an ordinary timetable.

That implies his suppers, water, play, strolling, and preparing times remain the same, even on the ends of the week!

Your dog doesn't have an inner schedule revealing to him it's Saturday, time to rest.

Five days you would be getting up at 6:00 AM to deal with him! See the example plans toward the end of this section.

When your dog is dependable, you can begin to shift the planned occasions marginally until you are back on "your" time.

FEED Positive Dinners.

Feed just a dry kibble at consistently planned occasions. Try not to leave nourishment down always for him to pick (as this is additionally called free bolstering).

You have to know when he has last eaten and how much he has eaten so you can time your potty breaks in like manner.

Water can be likewise offered at ordinary interims for youthful little dogs also, instead of leaving it down.

Persistently, or it tends to be allotted, so your dog doesn't swallow large sums. It ought to be offered more.

Frequently on hot days and after working out.

Make sure to restrict your dog when you can't watch him!

So how would i know when the dog needs to go out?
Attempt to prepare by knowing your very own dog's potty propensities. Most youthful pups tend to go out about

20 minutes in the wake of drinking a moderate measure of water; either directly after or inside 20 minutes of eating, after playing for any time allotment, in the wake of biting on a bone for a period, quickly after waking in the morning or following a snooze during the day.

Your primary responsibility is to realize when he needs to go so you can get your dog out to the right zone to take out before he has a slip-up in the house.

Your dog will likewise attempt to let you know by imparting through his non-verbal communication. Your dog will give this to you by sniffing at the ground all of a sudden, and in some cases, wildly hovering set up or halting play out of the blue for no obvious explanation.

More established dogs will regularly remain by the entryway driving outside for a couple of minutes before they choose they genuinely need to go, and you are not coming to allow them to out.

Each dog is somewhat extraordinary in his non-verbal communication when attempting to let you know "Gotta Go" so become more acquainted with your dog's interchanges signs so you can get him out on schedule.

Aversion, not revision, accelerates housetraining!

What do i do when my dog hits the nail on the head and goes in the right spot?

Acclaim him liberally as he is doing his business and give him a little treat within five seconds of him wrapping up.

At that point, take him back inside the house and play with him for three to four minutes. After, permit him 15 to 20 minutes of regulated opportunity in your home.

At the end, when you can't watch him anymore, at that point put him in his constrainment with a couple of toys to involve himself with.

Try not to push your dog out the entryway and anticipate that he should do his business on his claim!

You have to go with him to give him where and to ensure he does his business. He needs your assistance to learn house preparing accurately!

Attempt to get your dog out before he needs to go consistently. Don't hold up until you see him beginning to go in the house. Envision when he should proceed to get him out already!

When you have finished your doggy instruction and picked the ideal dog, you will discover there is a lot to do and a brief period to do it.

Here are your growing dog needs recorded arranged by desperation and positioned regarding significance.

- Family unit Manners (From the absolute first day your little dog returns home)

Housetraining, chew toy-preparing, and showing your dog options in contrast to recreational yapping are by a long shot the most squeezing things on your young dog's instructive plan.

From the very beginning, utilize errorless administration showing programs, involving restriction plans in addition to the liberal utilization of chew toys (Kong's, Scone Balls, and disinfected long bones) loaded down with kibble.

Essential conduct issues are so effectively preventable, yet they are the most well-known purposes behind individuals' disappointment with their dogs and the most widely recognized explanations behind dog killing.

Encouraging family habits ought to be your primary need the first day your pup gets home.

- Direness Rating

Family unit decorum is by a long shot the most squeezing thing on your new dog's instructive motivation.

In a situation that you need to abstain from irritating conduct issues, preparing must start the first day your young dog returns home.

- Significance Rating

Instructing family unit manners is critical. Little dogs immediately become unwelcome when their proprietors enable them to make house soiling, biting, yapping, burrowing, and related moves.

- Home Alone

(During the initial days your little dog is at home)

Unfortunately, the incensing pace of present-day local dodgem requires showing your little dog how to appreciate investing energy at home alone—not exclusively to guarantee your little guy to build up family behavior when solo, yet increasingly essential to keep your pup from getting restless in your nonattendance.

Ordinarily, these go inseparably because when dogs become on edge, they will, in general, bark, bite, burrow, and pee all the more now and again.

From the start, and particularly during his initial days in your home, your dog should be instructed how to engage himself discreetly, smoothly, and unhesitatingly.

Else he assuredly will turn out to be seriously focused when disregarded at home.

- Criticalness Rating

Training your puppy to appreciate his very own conversation certainly is the second direst thing on its instructive plan.

It is uncalled for to cover the dog with consideration and love during his first days or weeks at home, which possibly may expose the puppy to isolation when the grown-ups return to work and kids return to class.

During the initial barely days when you are around to screen your pup's conduct, instruct him to appreciate calm minutes bound to his young dog den or doggy sanctum.

Mainly make sure to give some word related treatment (stuffed chew toys) for your pup to occupy himself and agreeably take a break while you are away.

- Significance Rating

Setting up your little dog for time alone is critical both for your significant serenity, i.e., counteracting house soiling, biting, and yelping issues, and particularly for your pup's genuine feelings of serenity.

It is positively not a good time for the little guy to be over-dependent, pushed, and on edge.

- Socialization With Individuals

(Continuously, yet particularly before twelve weeks of age)

Numerous little dog preparing strategies center around showing your pup to appreciate the organization and activities of individuals.

Well-mingled hounds are sure and amicable, instead of dreadful and forceful. Show all relatives, guests, and outsiders how to get your little dog to come, sit, rests, turn over, and appreciate being taken care of for bits of kibble.

Living with an under-socialized dog can be disappointing, troublesome, and possibly dangerous.

For under-socialized hounds, life is unendurably upsetting.

- Direness Rating

Numerous individuals feel that little dog classes are for mingling dogs with individuals. Not obvious. Surely young dog classes give a helpful setting to mingled small dogs to keep associating with individuals.

In any case, young dogs must be all around associated with individuals before they to twelve weeks of age. The time-window for socialization shuts down at a quarter of a year of age.

Thus there is some desperation to sufficiently mingle your dog with individuals. During your little guy's first month at home, he needs to meet and interface decidedly with around one hundred distinct individuals!

- Significance Rating

Mingling your little dog to appreciate individuals is crucial—second, just in significance to your puppy, figure out how to repress the power of his.

Socialization should never end. Keep in mind, and your juvenile dog will start to dissocialize except if he keeps on meeting new individuals consistently. Walk your dog or extend your public activity at home.

- Dog Socialization

(Between a quarter of a year and eighteen weeks of age to build up dependable chomp restraint and always keen to keep up a friendship to different dogs)

When your dog turns three months old, the time has come to play make up for lost time as opposing dog socialization periods, now it's time for little dog classes, long strolls, and visits to hound parks.

Well-mingled dogs would prefer to play than chomp or battle. Also, well-mingled hounds, as a rule, chomp all the more delicately, if at any point they should nibble or battle.

- Desperation Rating

In a case that you might need to have a grown-up hound who appreciates the organization of different mutts, little dog classes and strolls are basic, mainly since numerous young dogs have been sequestered inside until they have been vaccinated against parvovirus and various doggy illnesses (by the most early at a quarter of a year of age).

- Significance Rating

It is difficult to rate the significance of dog socialization. Contingent upon the way of life of the proprietors, hound benevolence might be a redundant or essential quality.

During the situation that you may want to appreciate strolls with your grown-up hound, early socialization in little dog classes and dog parks is fundamental.

Interestingly, however, not many individuals walk their dogs. Though big dogs and urban dogs will, in general, be strolled regularly, little mutts and rural dogs are only "here and there" strolled.

Notwithstanding the ideal friendliness of your grown-up hound, dog play and particularly play-battling and play-gnawing during puppyhood, are significant for the improvement of chomp restraint and a delicate mouth.

Thus alone, little dog classes and outings to the dog park are the top needs at a quarter of a year of age.

- Sit and Settle Down Directions

(Start whenever you might want your puppy-dog to hear you out) If you show your dog only a few directions, they would need to be Sit and Settle Down. Think about all the naughty things your puppy-dog can't do when he is sitting.

- Desperation Rating

Not at all like socialization and chomp restraint, which must happen during puppyhood, you can show your dog to sit and settle down at any age, so there is no incredible desperation.

In any case, since it is so natural thus much enjoyable to show youthful pups, why not teach essential the habits the first day you bring your little dog home, or as right on time as four or five weeks if you are raising the litter?

The main desperation to encourage these straightforward and powerful control directions would be if at any point, your dog's shenanigans or movement level starts to disturb you. Sit or Settle Down practices will take care of most issues.

- Significance Rating

It is hard to rate the significance of essential habits. I like mutts that can appreciate being itself.

Then again, numerous individuals joyfully live with hounds with no conventional preparing at all. In a case that you believe your dog to be ideal for you, settle on your own decision.

In any case, you or others probably see your dog's conduct as irritating, why not show him how to carry on?

For sure, a straightforward sit avoids most of the disturbing conduct issues, including bouncing up, running through entryways, fleeing, annoying individuals, wasting time, pursuing the feline, and so on.

The rundown is long! It is such a significant amount to show your dog the proper behavior from the beginning, i.e., to show the one right way (e.g., to sit), as opposed to attempting to address the numerous things he fouls up.

In any case, it is unreasonable to jump on your dog's case for terrible habits in a case that he is just defying norms he didn't know existed.

- Nibble Restraint

(By eighteen weeks of age)

A delicate teeth is the absolute most significant quality for any dog. Ideally, your dog will never chew or battle, however, in case he does, settled nibble hindrance guarantees that your dog causes pretty much nothing of any harm.

Socialization is a progressing procedure of regularly enlarging experience and certainty fabricating that causes your little guy to efficiently deal with the difficulties and changes of ordinary grown-up life.

Be that as it may, it is difficult to set up your small dog for each conceivable inevitability, and on those extraordinary events when grown-up hounds are gravely harmed, alarmed, terrified, or upset, they only sometimes compose letters of protest.

Rather, hounds generally snarl and nibble, after which the degree of chomp restraint preparing from puppyhood predetermines the reality of the harm.

Grown-up hounds with unfortunate chomp hindrance only from time to time nibble, however when they do, the chomps quite often break the skin.

Nibble hindrance is one of the most misconstrued parts of social improvement in hounds (and different creatures). Numerous proprietors commit the cataclysmic error of preventing their pup from mouthing inside and out.

In the case that a dog isn't permitted to play-bite, he can't create substantial nibble hindrance. Puppies are brought into the world virtual gnawing machines with needle-sharp teeth, so they get the hang of gnawing harms before they build up the jaw strength to cause apparent damage.

Be that as it may, they can't figure out how to restrain the power of their chomps if they are never permitted to play-nibble and play-battle.

Nibble hindrance preparing involves first encouraging the young dog to dynamically hinder the power of his chomps until little dog play.

Conclusion

Closing Credits

The ideas, steps, advice, procedures shared in this book **TRAIN YOUR PUPPY:**

(A Practical and Effective Training Manual that Teaches You How To Literally Hack Your Puppy's Brain to Make Him Do Anything You Want. Even If You Don't Think You Can Do It) are not only to be read but as well put into practice.

Take the steps enlisted in training your puppy to become the adult dog you always wanted.

CPSIA information can be obtained
at www.ICGtesting.com
Printed in the USA
LVHW052148181120
672055LV00034B/1231